Business Report Guides

Business Report Guides

Routine and Nonroutine Reports and Policies, Procedures, and Instructions

Dorinda Clippinger

BEP BUSINESS EXPERT PRESS

Business Report Guides: Routine and Nonroutine Reports and Policies, Procedures, and Instructions

Copyright © Business Expert Press, LLC, 2019.

First published in 2019 by
Business Expert Press, LLC
222 East 46th Street, New York, NY 10017
www.businessexpertpress.com

ISBN-13: 978-1-63157-417-7 (paperback)
ISBN-13: 978-1-63157-418-4 (e-book)

Business Expert Press Corporate Communication Collection

Collection ISSN: 2156-8162 (print)
Collection ISSN: 2156-8170 (electronic)

Cover and interior design by Exeter Premedia Services Private Ltd., Chennai, India

First edition: 2019

10 9 8 7 6 5 4 3 2 1

Printed in the United States of America.

Abstract

Business Report Guides: Routine and Nonroutine Reports and Policies, Procedures, and Instructions: a warehouse of how-to information for creating many types of reports. The broad scope of this book includes reports that managers create often; reports they may generate occasionally; and organizational policies, procedures, and work instructions. This book is for you if you are (1) a business manager or other professional whose career involves generating reports for others in and outside your organization or (2) an MBA candidate or an upper-level student in any professional field.

This practical book includes guidelines—with examples and complete illustrations—for generating over 20 diverse reports in 12 categories; principles for designing digital and paper report forms and for planning, organizing, and writing effective narrative reports, along with options for formatting reports, including e-mail, letter, manuscript, and memo formats.

Business Report Guides also clarifies the characteristics of policies, procedures, processes, and work instructions and the significance of each within organizations. In addition, it offers considerations for both print and digital employee manual content, design, and acknowledgment, with emphasis on the legal considerations involved.

Lists of software and service provider options to make reporting more efficient and effective round out this useful book.

The crisp writing style, bullet points, and many realistic examples and full-report visuals give you essential information quickly. Chapter summaries include checklists. *Business Report Guides* gives you how-to information you can use now—and refer to frequently throughout your career.

Keywords

acknowledgment of receipt; backgrounder; best practices; digital employee handbook; meeting agenda; meeting summary (minutes); overview; process map; production report; progress report; proposals; social media news release; trip (travel) report; white paper; work instructions

Contents

Preface

Business Report Guides: Routine and Nonroutine Reports and Policies, Procedures, and Instructions is designed to help business managers, MBA candidates, and upper-level college students develop business reporting skills. Think of reports as organized, objective presentations of facts, experiences, or observations used in the decision-making process. Some reports are short, simple messages; others are much longer and more complex. This book is the ideal tool for mastering many kinds of reports.

The main purposes of *Business Report Guides* are (1) to help readers tweak their skills when writing familiar reports and (2) to approach unfamiliar reports systematically and confidently. The book offers recognized guidelines for creating various reports while promoting efficiency by bringing in the latest software applications and services. Numerous examples and full-report visuals help ensure readers' complete understanding.

In three chapters, readers receive practical solutions to a range of reporting situations that professionals are likely to encounter at some point:

- Chapter 1 covers routine reports common to professional activity—how to create them, use them, and design standard forms for them.
- Chapter 2 focuses on nonroutine reports, including those related to employment, recommendations, publicity, marketing, and information summary. Since some reports require writing persuasively, the chapter discusses and demonstrates persuasion and the common logical fallacies that undermine it.
- Chapter 3 presents strategies for developing and using policies, procedures, work instructions, and employee manuals.

Business Report Guides can be your go-to handbook for years to come. Reading through it in a couple hours, you can pick up plenty of information that you can apply immediately. Then keep this book handy and refer to it as needs arise in your future.

Acknowledgments

I am grateful to Dr. Debbie DuFrene, the expert editor who transformed my drafts into this reader-friendly book. Also, I am indebted to Dr. Shirley Kuiper, whose earlier writings and vision underpin this publication. Thanks also to my husband William Jewell for his continual affection and support. During my half century of teaching, publishing, research, and business ownership, many students and associates influenced my thinking about educating for business, business communication, and other business practices. I owe a huge debt to them.

Please send your suggestions for improving future editions.

CHAPTER 1

Writing Routine Reports

A business career usually involves a variety of simple reports. A simple report (sometimes called a short report) does not require an extensive search for the necessary information. In many instances, you will recall from memory the principal data for the report. In other situations, you may refer to a meeting summary, a file folder, notes written during a conference, or e-mails or texts sent to you by co-workers or clients.

Although the data-gathering method may be relatively simple, the resulting report still fits the definition of business reports: organized, objective presentations of observations, experiences, or facts used in an organization's decision-making process. Simple reports—those you write and those written by others—influence your job performance and career advancement.

Simple reports can be further classified as routine and nonroutine reports. A routine report is one that you prepare as a part of your normal work assignment. Its purpose is to keep people informed of how you are accomplishing your regular duties. A weekly sales report is an example of a routine report. That report and others are demonstrated in this chapter.

In contrast, a nonroutine report deals with situations that are exceptions to your daily activities and responsibilities. For example, you may be authorized to grant a potentially lucrative customer a larger-than-normal discount on an initial order. However, since that is not the normal sales procedure, the situation may call for a report notifying your sales manager of your actions. Chapter 2 presents examples of nonroutine reports.

Using Standard Forms

When an organization requires frequent reporting of the same categories of information, efficiency is gained by developing a standard form for that report, whether it is used internally (inside the company) or externally (sent to customers or clients).[1] For example, most health insurance organizations send reports to insured parties indicating how a claim for payment of medical services has been processed. Since an insurance company processes many such claims each day and reports the same categories of information to each customer, using a standard form expedites the reporting process. Examples of internal reports include those related to activity on delivery routes, repairs or use of equipment and vehicles, or production and sales activity (see Figure 1.1). In fact, practically any type of routine report can be put on a form.

Business Form Sources

The word form may bring images of preprinted papers to mind. Paper forms from a commercial printer—flat, plain-paper forms and snap-out, multiple-copy sets—are still common office supplies, but they are not the only forms available. Figure 1.1 shows a form template created with spreadsheet software (Microsoft Excel in this case). In addition, Excel offers several generic form templates that can be adapted to specific uses. Of course, form templates may be printed in quantity or converted to PDF and printed individually as needed; but form templates are meant to be filled in at your keyboard, with the aid of built-in formulas in worksheet templates.

In a company, a template form should be easily accessible to everyone who needs to use it: saved to individual desktop computers or accessible through a company's network of computers and mobile devices.[2] These networks—also called intranets and content management systems (CMS)—often contain form libraries, collections of all the forms used in the organization. Usually, these forms involve content controls, such as check boxes, text boxes, date pickers, and drop-down lists, to speed up form completion.[3]

A more advanced way to create forms is to use forms automation software, either installed on company computers (standalone or networked) or accessed on the web. These packages are designed for business process management (BPM)—a system for making workflow more effective, efficient, and flexible at achieving organizational goals.

Weekly Sales Report
Form S185

Salesperson:	Olivia Rutledge	Week Ending:	10/5/2019
Location:	Baltimore – Region 3	Report Date:	10/7/2019

Days	Total Hours			Sales Numbers				Revenue (Definite Future Bookings)			
	In Sales Office	Outside Sales Office	Non-Sales Work*	In-Office Visits & Tours	Outside Calls	File Phone Calls	New Account Phone Calls	Guest Rooms	Food & Beverage	Meeting Room Rental	Revenue Totals
Monday	6.00	1.00	0.75	3	35	21	2	$ 5,000	$ 3,300	$ -	$ 8,300
Tuesday	5.00	2.00	1.00	9	40	33	45	$ 10,540	$ 7,060	$ 3,000	$ 20,600
Wednesday	8.00	0.00	0.00	10	23	45	60	$ 11,455	$ 7,675	$ 3,000	$ 22,130
Thursday	5.00	3.00	0.00	17	0	39	75	$ 10,875	$ 7,285	$ 3,000	$ 21,160
Friday	3.00	3.00	1.00	21	39	33	26	$ 9,880	$ 6,620	$ -	$ 16,500
Saturday	0.00	3.00	0.00	0	0	0	0	$ -	$ -	$ -	$ -
Sunday	0.00	1.00	0.00	0	0	0	0	$ -	$ -	$ -	$ -
Totals	27.00	13.00	2.75	60	137	171	208	$ 47,750	$ 31,940	$ 9,000	$ 88,690
Goals	20.00	20.00	0.00	75	170	175	200	$ 51,500	$ 34,500	$ 3,000	$ 89,000
Variance	7.00	-7.00	2.75	-15	-33	-4	8	$ (3,750)	$ (2,560)	$ 6,000	$ (310)

*Explain if over 2 hours in one day.

SOFT Notes

Highlight your

Successes

Opportunities

Failures

Threats

Directions: Submit this form to the hotel manager by 3 on Monday for your sales activity the previous week (Sunday through Saturday). SOFT Notes are optional but appreciated.

Salesperson's signature:

Manager's signature:

Figure 1.1 Form report of sales activity (Form created in Microsoft Excel 365.)

Most of the following forms applications can be installed on an organization's computers or deployed on the web. Software features and pricing plans vary widely. To find the right combination of features and price for your organization, consult a software reviewer, such as Capterra (www.capterra.com).

Forms applications:

- Canvas Mobile Forms (https://gocanvas.com/content/home)
- Dokmee Capture Scanning Solution (https://dokmee.com/en-us/products/capture.aspx)
- Fat Finger (https://seeforge.com)
- Forms Automation Software (https://form.com)
- Forms on Fire—Mobile (https://formsonfire.com)
- Intellect Forms (https://intellect.com)
- Quik! Forms (http://efficienttech.com)
- Snappii Mobile Apps (https://snappii.com)

Business Form Design

For starters when designing a paper or on-screen form, you should know the purpose of the form and who will use it. Then, as the designer, ensure accurate completion, facilitate navigation, and make the form attractive (including forms for in-house use only).

Following these guides will enable you to meet your objectives.[4]

- *Keep the form simple.* Arrange data fields in logical sequence (left to right and top to bottom) and provide a clear caption for each data field.
- *Include instructions for completing each form.* Even if use of the form seems obvious to you, explain concisely who needs to complete the form, how to complete it, and what to do upon finishing the form. These directions

will help ensure accurate completion by everyone using the form, including first-time users. Note that these instructions should appear on the form itself, not on a separate sheet.

- *If the form contains columns, provide short, descriptive column headings.* If words must be shortened, use only standard abbreviations. In addition, avoid crowding; put reasonable spacing between columns.
- *Provide enough space for entering data.* Make the data entry positions obvious and allow adequate horizontal and vertical space for the entries. If needed, add a page to prevent overcrowding.
- *Observe the principles of graphic design*, especially alignment, contrast, proximity, and repetition.
  1. *Vertical alignment of elements makes a form attractive and clear.*
  2. *Contrast helps users navigate a form.* Create contrast with font sizes and styles and the use of shaded and unshaded areas.
  3. *Proximity gives a form logic*, or coherence. Use the principle of proximity by placing related data fields together and placing space between unrelated fields.
  4. *Repetition unifies parts of a form.* If you use a contrast element, such as bold text, for a column heading or a key word, use bold for several more column headings or key words.

Figures 1.2a and 1.2b (p. 7) contrast a poorly designed form with one that observes these design principles.

- *If possible, use checkboxes to simplify choices.* Always include an option for data that does not match a specific checkbox.
- *On paper forms, do not use boxes for individual letters*—unless the form will be read by electronic scanners. In that case, provide boxes roughly 0.25 in. (5 mm) square.
- *Include a heading and form number on every form.* Besides the full name of the form, show the organization's name or logo and the form number in the heading.

Penworthy

1306 Hampton St., Chambersburg, PA 17201-1425

Phone: 717-555-2432

FAX: 717-555-2430

To: Cc:

FAX: PAGES:

From:

SUBJECT:

¤ Urgent   ¤ For review   ¤ Please reply   ¤ Please
recycle

>>>

<<<<<<<<<<<<<<<<<<<<<<<<<<<<<<<<<<<<<<<<<<<<<<<<<<<<<<<

Figure 1.2 (a) Poorly designed business form

Note: Oftentimes, form numbers appear in a small font in the bottom left or right corner, making them hard to locate. The accurate name and form number are vital when an organization needs to catalog many different forms.

Planning a Narrative Report

In the absence of a standard form, business people write their routine reports, mainly as e-mail and interoffice memoranda (memos). All good reports start out with careful planning.[5] Your plan will start with articulating your purpose and what it is you want to accomplish. What is your general purpose: production, innovation, goodwill, what? Then, specifically, what do you want the receiver(s) of your report to do?

FAX

Penworthy

Phone: 717-555-2432
FAX: 717-555-2440
Address: 1306 Hampton St.
           Chambersburg, PA 17201-1425

Date	From
To	CC
FAX	Pages
Phone	☐ URGENT ☐ Please Reply
Subject	☐ Please Comment ☐ For Review

Figure 1.2 (b) Well-designed business form (Form created in Microsoft Word 365.)

Next, you will need to analyze your audiences—both your immediate reader and possible others who might be brought into the thought process—and what they want and need from the report. Another important element in your planning is to consider the context, or overall circumstances, in which you are writing and whether the writing style should be formal or informal. Then you will decide on the content needed, how to organize the report, and how to deliver it.

Two basic strategies for most reports are the direct and the indirect structure. The direct structure is based on the deductive style of reasoning: from general to specific. Indirect structure is patterned after inductive reasoning, which moves from specific examples or facts to generalized conclusions. The appropriate strategy for any report depends on its specific purpose, content, and context. Generally, a simple report fits the following description.

- *Purpose:* inform a decision maker about some aspect of your work or work-related activity
- *Content:* familiar to the report's reader because he or she is acquainted with your work and activities
- *Context:* reader expects to get your report; needs little or no explanation to understand it

This description suggests that readers of your routine reports will need little psychological preparation for the main point because it is an expected or easy-to-accept message. In other words, the direct structure is appropriate for most routine reports. (The indirect structure is most fitting when the reader requires background details before being able to understand or accept the gist of the message.)

Direct (Deductive) Structure

As noted, a report written in direct structure begins with the main point (a generalization), which is followed by supporting data (the facts that justify the generalization). The following example demonstrates the direct (deductive) structure. The main point or general statement ("By targeting new clients … to increase revenues to my territory by about 33%.") precedes the detailed facts about the new clients and established clients.

Writer's objective: Report personal productivity for the month.
Subject: Sales and Delivery Activity, April 2019
By targeting new clients and providing prompt service to established clients, I have been able in April to increase revenues to my territory by about 33%. Here is a summary of my activity.
New Clients

Prospects contacted	63
New clients from those contacts	19

Total revenues related to new clients	$23,401.50
Total pickups	123
Total deliveries	51
Established Clients	
Total pickups	326
Total deliveries	215
Total revenues from established clients	$70,550.75
Total Revenues	$93,952.25

Organization Patterns

For ordering report paragraphs, rely on these nine commonly used organization patterns. Select the pattern that seems best suited—the most natural fit—to your report. To help you choose an appropriate organization pattern, list the report content, using keywords, short phrases, or both. Next, ask yourself this vital question: What order of presentation will best help the report's reader(s) grasp its message? Then, rearrange the listed words and phrases to create an informal outline to use as you write a draft.

Chronological Pattern

Chronological order uses time as the report's central organizer. This pattern is especially appropriate when time is an essential ingredient for understanding the basis of a request or for fulfilling that request. Any time units—minutes, hours, days, weeks, months, years, or eras—relevant to the report may be used. The following example illustrates the chronological pattern.

Objective: To inform the reader of target dates for completing the remaining steps in a project.

The Nguyen team is well on the road to improving the efficiency of emergency room procedures here at City Central Hospital.

The team plans to have our patient flow coordination plan fully operational on July 1, the beginning of the next fiscal year. That timing will enable us to do an effective cost-benefit analysis after one year of operation. Please note these important dates.

June 15	Complete hiring of Patient Flow Coordinators
June 20	Complete training of PFCs
June 21–25	Conduct trail run of new flow system, including use of electronic checklists by medical personnel
June 25–29	Identify and implement any changes resulting from trial run
June 30	Have all procedures in place and personnel confident about following them

Problem-Solution

As the name implies, the problem-solution pattern describes a problem and a proposed solution. Using direct structure, the request would precede details of the problem. This order works when the problem and proposed solution can be stated concisely and are likely to receive little objection. When dealing with a complex problem, you may find the inductive style more fitting because it gives you greater latitude to describe the details of the problem and the reasons for the proposed solution. Here is an example of problem-solution order.

Objective: To report a problem and request approval of a likely solution.

Problem: Several factors contributed to construction delays during the past two months:

1. The supplier of plumbing supplies delivered substandard materials. The construction site chief, Barry Benson, insisted on the quality specified in the contract. Those materials were delivered two weeks later.

2. As you know, our policy calls for paying skilled-labor crews only when they are on the job. Therefore, Benson could not pay the plumbing crew while waiting for the materials. So that crew moved to another construction project.

3. Owing to high demand for and low supply of skilled-labor crews in the Edgewater area, we lost another week while Benson tried to

hire a new plumbing crew. Obviously, some phases of construction could not be completed until the plumbing was installed.

Solution: Benson asked that he be allowed to pay skilled-labor crews for up to one week of waiting time when delays are caused by shortages of materials. He accepts that construction crews normally are not paid for weather-related delays. But in a fairly tight labor market, we risk losing good crews if we refuse to pay them for other delays.

Cause-Effect

When using the cause-effect pattern, the writer identifies and discusses conditions (causes) and a predicted outcome (effect) of those conditions. (This pattern, too, reflects inductive structure because it moves from specific facts to generalizations based on those facts.) The cause-effect pattern is appropriate when you want to report your perception of a direct relationship between two or more events. The following example uses cause-effect organization.

Objective: To justify an investment in retrofitting hotel rooms to meet hypoallergenic standards

Three months ago, we gave a contract to EnviroRooms to convert the fifth floor of our hotel into a hypoallergenic zone. The work was completed on time and on budget. We are already seeing a return on that investment. The bookings for the Thanksgiving weekend were 10% above last year's bookings. Most of that increase can be attributed to the number of reservations for hypoallergenic rooms.

Spatial Pattern

The spatial pattern is appropriate any time your data can be presented logically in terms of geographic units. Those units may be as large as continents or nations or as small as areas of a parking lot or a room. You may, for instance, wish to analyze the layout of an office, parking lot assignments, productivity by sales districts, or market potential by countries.

The spatial pattern would be appropriate for presenting data analysis, conclusions, or recommendations for each of those reports. The following sample shows the spatial pattern in the presentation of recommendations.

Objective: To meet customer-service needs effectively in all areas of the city

As requested, my project team analyzed customer assistance calls, complaints about customer assistance, and potential needs for customer assistance in our market area. Based on that analysis, the team recommends the following changes in service personnel.

Central City	Add one service consultant
Northeast	Add two service consultants and one technician
Northwest	Add two service technicians
Southwest	Reassign one technician from this district to the Southeast district
Southeast	Assign one technician from the Southwest district and add one service consultant

Topical

In topical organization, information is ordered around major topics of discussion. For instance, a research report divided into Findings, Conclusions, and Recommendations is organized topically. To be more meaningful, however, topical headings should identify the factors or elements involved. For instance, a report presenting the results of a survey to determine preferences for employee benefits could be structured properly in terms of the major categories of benefits, such as medical insurance, retirement plans, child or elder care, and profit sharing. The following example shows headings in a credit union report arranged by topic.

Objective: To present credit union performance on major measures of operating success
Subject: Credit Union Performance, 2019

Distribution of Consumer Savings

Text details the distribution of consumer savings among credit union customers. Xxxxx xxxxxx xxx xxxxxxx xxxx xx xxxxxxxx xxx xxxxx. Xxx xxxxx xxxxxxx xx xxx xxxxx. Xxxxx. ...

Composition of Savings

Text explains the makeup of savings. Xxx xxxxx xxxxxxx xx xxx xxxxx. Xxxxx xxxxxx xxx xxxxxxx xxxx xx xxxxxxxx xxx xxxxx. Xxx xxxxx xxxxxxx xx xxx xxxxx. Xxxxx xxx xxxx.

Share of Installment Credit Outstanding by Selected Lenders

Text describes the proportion of outstanding installment loans at certain lending institutions. Xxxxx xxxxxx xxx xxxxxxx xxxx xx xxxxxxxx xxx xxxxx. Xxx xxxxx xxxxxxx xx xxx xxxxx.

Share of Auto Loans Outstanding by Selected Lenders

Text states the proportion of outstanding auto loans at specific lending institutions. Xxxx xxxxxxxxx xxx xxxxxxxxxx xx. Xxxxxxxxxx xxxxxxxxxxx xxxxx xx xxxxxxx xxxxxxx. Xxxxx ....

Average Loan Rates by Credit Union Asset Size

Text addresses the topic of loan rates in relation to size of the lending institution. Xxxxx xxxxxx xxx xxxxxxx xxxx xx xxxxxxxx xxx xxxxx. Xxx xxxxx xxxxxxx xx xxx xxxxx. Xxx xxxxxxx.

Comparison or Contrast

The comparison and contrast patterns examine two or more items in terms of common criteria. Comparison implies examining the qualities of items to discover similarities. Contrasting focuses primarily on differences between or among items.

Assume, for instance, that you are leading a project team in your organization. The team is charged with creating a report for company executives. These upper-level managers want to encourage middle managers to pursue an MBA degree by offering an incentive. The purpose of your report is to provide an objective tool for comparing three MBA programs. The team has determined the criteria by which the programs will be evaluated: admission standards, cost, program requirements, quality of faculty, and reputation among the business professionals your organization

serves. The team's report could be structured suitably around those criteria, showing how the programs are similar or different on each criterion.
One organizational pattern would evaluate each program on all criteria,
as shown in the following example.

Objective: To compare three MBA programs
Program A
    Admission Standards
    Cost
    Requirements
    Faculty
    Reputation
Program B
    Admission Standards
    Cost
    Requirements
    Faculty
    Reputation
Program C
    Admission Standards
    Cost
    Requirements
    Faculty
    Reputation

Another organizational pattern would compare all colleges on each
criterion, as shown in this example.

Admission Standards
    Program A
    Program B
    Program C
Cost
    Program A
    Program B

Program C
Requirements
    Program A
    Program B
    Program C
Faculty
    Program A
    Program B
    Program C
Reputation
    Program A
    Program B
    Program C

Combination

As you may have inferred, some reports use two or more of the organizers discussed: the combination pattern. The report in Figure 1.11, for example, is organized by topics, represented by bold headings. That report also uses the chronological pattern, reviewing actions of the past three months, referring to other incidents in order of occurrence, and providing a list of target dates for future events.

Choosing a Writing Style

After planning and outlining a report, you are ready to write a draft. For simple reports, your first draft usually will be your final draft. To help ensure that ideal, decide on a writing style before you draft. Always empathize with readers, considering their information needs and ego needs, and keep the context and your purpose in mind.[6]

Your writing style will be further defined by three attributes:
  • *Tone* refers to the attitude the writer conveys about the message and the reader. For example, a report may be appeasing or defensive, passive or persuasive, personal or

impersonal, polite or peremptory, and positive or negative. Note the appeasing, persuasive, personal, polite, and positive tone of reports throughout the chapter

- *Degree of formality* refers to wording that conveys how well the writer and reader are acquainted. Use of first names; contractions; first- and second-person pronouns, such as I, me, we, us, and you; and colloquial expressions characterize informal style. The absence of these elements denotes formal style.

- As you review sample routine reports, you will see first-person pronouns used in some of them—an individual's productivity report or a team's progress report, for example. Otherwise, the writing style is formal. The reason: The writer took secondary readers into consideration. Likewise, your routine reports may pass among many readers, some of whom you may not even know, and then be filed for future use by other people. Therefore, a formal style is generally preferable.

- *Objectivity* involves reporting all relevant information— even if the reader would have preferred a different outcome. The word also includes expressing information without bias or emotion—but with suitable confidence. In the sample reports, notice that strengths and weaknesses, successes and failures, progress and problems are reported with equal objectivity.

Qualities of Effective Reports

Effective reports are understood by the receiver as the originator intended, and they influence the receiver to act as the report's writer desired. As the report maker, your objectives will be most likely achieved if they correspond with the needs and objectives of the recipient. An effective report involves the following qualities.

- *Empathy*. Report shows that writer is sensitive to and vicariously experiencing the needs or feelings of the report reader.

- *Accuracy.* Report conveys correct information through precise number use (and visuals in some cases), careful word choice, and exact spelling, grammar, and punctuation.
- *Completeness.* Report includes all essential information, enabling the reader to interpret the information as the writer intended.
- *Conciseness.* Report uses the fewest words necessary to achieve the other qualities.
- *Clarity.* Report is easy to read and understand. Text flows (moves continuously in one direction).

These qualities are present in the e-mail message shown in Figure 1.3. Notice the following qualities of Figure 1.3.

- This e-mail fits the definition of a report: It is an organized, objective presentation of fact, and it is written to influence action.
- The organizational structure is evidenced by headings as well as numbered and bulleted items. (The structure is direct; the organization pattern is problem-solution.)

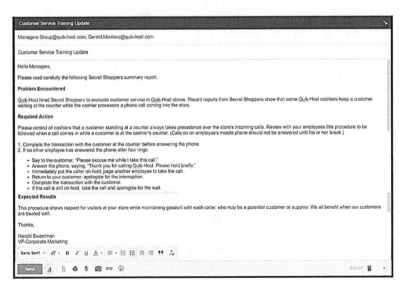

Figure 1.3 Effective report qualities demonstrated

- Beginning with the description of a problem adds to the accuracy and completeness of the data, helping the reader understand the importance of the requested action.
- The organization and format help the reader focus on the main points (skim value), thereby showing empathy for the reader.
- The tone of the message, courteous yet firm, also demonstrates empathy.
- The language is clear and concrete, avoiding such trite expressions as "It has come to our attention that ..."
- The simple (familiar) words and relatively short sentences and paragraphs contribute to clarity.
- The mix of simple and complex sentences makes for clear, interesting reading.
- The bullet items convey completeness by showing exactly what to say when carrying out the requested action.
- Structural consistency also aids clarity. Each two-word heading describes the content below it. The bullet items are constructed very similarly (called parallel form). All are complete sentences with action verbs at or near the beginning (Say, Answer, put, Return, Complete, take).
- Technical accuracy—no errors in grammar, punctuation, spelling, and word choice—also aids clarity. *Note*: For proofing your reports to ensure technical accuracy, use the guides in Appendix A.
- The requested action is written in clear, concise language, providing a concrete procedure to be followed.
- The closing comment about expected results again demonstrates empathy, noting that the requested action will benefit the e-mail receiver, not just the sender.

Formatting Routine Reports

Formatting a report is comparable to packaging a product. An effective format will entice the receiver to read the report; lead the reader effortlessly through the information presented; maintain the reader's interest; and, ideally, stimulate the reader to respond to the report as you had hoped. Applying the following basic guides will help your readers scan your reports, quickly determine content, and focus attention on specific information.[7]

Text Formatting Guides

Applying the following guides will help your reader scan your report, quickly determine its content, and focus attention on specific information. Apply these guides to any written report.

Spacing

Most business reports omit blank lines between text lines (called single spacing). *Note*: Multiple spacing is often used in place of strict single spacing because Multiple is the default setting in Microsoft Word. Multiple spacing puts a tiny space between text lines, making text more open and easier to read. In Word 365, the default spacing is Multiple 1.08; in an earlier version of Word, Multiple 1.15. In everyday usage, these default settings are still referred to as single spacing. However, instead of using default settings automatically, determine the preferences of your readers (your employer or other readers); and change the settings to meet their expectations.

A small amount of blank space roughly equivalent to a line of text separates paragraphs of single-spaced reports. Generally, single-spaced paragraphs have no paragraph indentations but should always have one or more blank lines below each paragraph.

Fonts

Your selection of font, font style, and font size affects the appearance and readability of your report. The main goal of fonts is to create a document that is consistent, harmonious, and balanced. Too much variety can be distracting to a reader.

Font refers to the shape or design of letters and characters. As the fonts in Figure 1.4 show, some fonts are much more intricate—and often less readable—than others.

Serif Fonts	Sans Serif Fonts
Cambria, regular	Calibri, regular
Cambria, bold	**Calibri, bold**
Cambria, italics	*Calibri, italics*
Palatino Linotype, regular	Dubai, regular
Palatino Linotype, bold	**Dubai, bold**
Palatino Linotype, italics	*Dubai, italics*
Times New Roman, regular	Verdana, regular
Times New Roman, bold	**Verdana, bold**
Times New Roman, italics	*Verdana, italics*

Figure 1.4 Comparative fonts and font styles

Fonts are identified as serif or sans serif. Serif refers to the fine lines that cross the bottom and top of a letter. (Notice the lines at the bottom of *f, k, l, m, n,* and *r* in the previous sentence.) Sans serif fonts do not have lines at the bottom and top of letters.

Along with choosing a font, consider font style. Most of your report text should be produced in regular or plain style. Bold, italic, bold-italic, and underlining may be used sparingly for emphasis or to clarify the text. As an example, bold is often used for headings and subheadings and italics for names of publications or other emphasis. Limit underlining to subheadings, if you like underlined subheadings, and a few words in paragraphs. Readers recognize words by their shapes; underlining tends to obscure the descending portions of letters like g, j, p, and y as shown here: g, j, p, y.

Consider font size, too. Size 10 may be too small for some readers, but you might occasionally use it when you want to limit the pages in a report or shrink a report to one page. Any size larger than 14 is considered a display font and should be reserved for headings. Using anything larger than 12 for the main text may give the impression that you are trying to pad your report. In e-mail and memos, use one size font only.

Note: Again, check the default font in your word processing program. Microsoft Word 365, for example, uses Calibri, a sans serif font, as the default setting. Traditionally serif fonts, such as Cambria and Times New Roman, were used for the main text of printed reports because the serifs create a line to lead a reader's eye from left to right. Thus, serif text is easier to read on the printed page. On an e-mail screen (browser), however, a sans serif font, such as Calibri and Verdana are easier to read. If the default setting in your software does not correspond with the standards set by your employer, change the default settings to meet expectations.

Emphasis Techniques

When you want to emphasize certain information in a report, you may use one of several emphasis techniques, such as full capitalization (ALL CAPS), bold style, italics style, bulleted lists, numbered lists, and shading. The following list will guide you in using these emphasis techniques effectively.

- Use ALL-CAPS in short spans, such as a main heading or a few key words in a long paragraph. LONG STRINGS OF CAPITALIZED TEXT ARE HARD TO READ. Additionally, using all uppercase letters has come to be equated with shouting. E-mail protocols, for instance, discourage use of all-capital letters except for headings or occasional emphasis within a message.
- Use bold in moderation. Apply it to a few words or phrases up to a short sentence or two that are altogether worthy of emphasis.
- Likewise, use italics sparingly. When too many things are emphasized, nothing receives appropriate attention. Besides italicizing coined words and the titles of complete published and artistic works that contain subdivisions, use italics when you want *readers to slow down and read more carefully*.

Grouping and bulleting or numbering closely related items focuses attention on that information. To group items effectively, follow these guides.

- Use an introductory sentence or phrase to unify the group. The sentence immediately preceding this list is an example of such a sentence. Include at least two or three items in your list. Logically, you cannot have a group of one.
- Write all items in parallel grammatical form. Case in point: Each item in this list begins with an imperative verb and is followed by additional information.

- Use bullets if order of the items is irrelevant. Use numbers if the list represents a ranking of importance or a sequence, such as the steps in a procedure.
- Choose one bullet style for all lists in a document. Mostly use a traditional bullet style (large, solid circle or square), reserving more exotic characters for special reports, such as newsletters.
- Put the same space between bulleted or numbered items that appears between regular paragraphs.
- Align bulleted or numbered items at the paragraph point.
- Use the hanging indentation style for bulleted and numbered items. This style aligns the text 0.25 in. or 0.5 in. to the right of the bullet or number. *Note*: Omit this guide for e-mail reports.

Headings

Headings should represent the outline of your report and guide the reader through its content. Simple reports like those in this chapter involve just one level of heading. In longer, more complex reports that have main divisions and sub-divisions, headings must convey the relationship of those sections.

Each heading should be close to the text it covers. The space between a heading and the text to which it applies should be the same as the space between paragraphs. And if a heading appears on the last line of a page, use a page break or spacing to force it to the top of the next page.

As you study the illustrations of reports in this book, note how these basic guides for spacing, fonts, headings, and emphasis are applied, or at least simulated. In addition, observe the following specific guides for reports in e-mail and memo formats.

Specific Formatting Guides

Report formatting refers to appearance and arrangement of individual elements in reports. Historically, paper-based reports involved three main formats—manuscript, memo, and letter. Each format involved conventions that most business people used in producing their reports and expected to find in the reports they received. In fact, the standards for manuscripts, memos, and letters remain largely the same today.

However, with the rise of electronic media (including e-mail, slide decks, and web pages) for delivering reports to audiences, rigid formatting rules have given way to guidelines for producing reports in each medium. (*Note*: In this chapter, narrative reports appear in e-mail and memo formats. Business letter format is introduced in Chapter 2, and manuscript format is shown in Appendix B [pp. 199–202]).

The following two guidelines apply equally to all report formats.

- Choose a simple, functional design. You will impress readers most by providing just the information they need in a way that makes it easy for them to find and understand it. In any format, an overly elaborate design may give readers the impression that you did not pay enough attention to content.
- Know what formatting decisions you can or may make. Your company, for example, may already have a standard report format that everyone in the organization is supposed to use.

You may be expected to use certain templates in your word processing or presentation software so that documents in a series look alike; or if someone has adapted or created a template for reports like the one you are writing; you may be expected to use it.

Organizations often use wikis for internal reporting, especially progress, or status, reports. In addition, organizations often use blogs for reports requiring immediate written feedback from report readers, such as evaluation and recommendation reports.[8]

E-mail Format

Brief internal reports—like the one in Figure 1.3—may be delivered by e-mail. E-mail has a couple of obvious advantages over other formats:

It can be distributed quickly to single or multiple readers, and e-mail reports can be filed electronically or printed and filed on paper for future reference.

The format in Figure 1.3 shows standard e-mail headings: receivers' address (To heading), the topic (Subject heading), and the recipient of a copy (Cc heading). Another copy option is Bcc (the "B" stands for blind), used to conceal the identity of a copy recipient and to prevent a long list of e-mail addresses at the top of a message. (*Note*: The use of two c's is a carryover from the past. Originally, cc stood for carbon copy, a duplicate document created on a typewriter by inserting carbon paper between sheets of plain paper. Later, cc stood for courtesy copy. In the future, expect the cc convention to give way to a single c or the word copy.) Once sent, of course, the e-mail will show the sender's address (From heading) as well as when the message was mailed (Date and Time headings). The subject field is vital to an e-mail report's success, so always specify the topic of your report.

Following these guidelines will help you write effective subject lines.[9]

- Fill in the subject field before entering your message. Doing so keeps you from forgetting. E-mail with a blank subject field is often deleted or lost—and is always irritating to the recipient who must open it to determine its subject.
- Enter a few words that precisely describe your topic. Place the most important words at the beginning, omitting fillers. While a typical mailbox shows 60 characters in the subject field, a mobile device may show half that number or fewer, so keep it short. Include keywords that the recipient might use to filter and search for your report later.
- Use combined Caps and lowercase, which is easier to read at a glance than ALL CAPS.
- When you receive a reply that in turn requires a reply from you, be sure to change the subject line to match your new message.

As shown in Figure 1.3, a salutation, or greeting, above the e-mail message is appropriate. A greeting confirms for the recipient that he or she is the intended reader of the e-mail. Since e-mail is inherently informal, a greeting such as Dear Ms. Bissell is usually too formal. But any of these salutations is suitable, depending on how well you know the individual recipient: Dear Jean, Jean Bissell, or just Jean.

In ongoing dialogues, you may consider deleting the greeting after the initial exchange, but if you are writing to a client or to someone in your organization who is senior to you, wait until that person omits the salutation before doing so.[10] Additional guidelines follow.

- As noted earlier, use content headings to show how your e-mail report is organized.
- Use a sans serif font, which, on a computer screen, is easier to read than a serif font. And use a medium-sized (12) or larger (14) font. The larger font is considerate of people who read e-mail on their mobile phones. Headings can be even larger (16). But do keep this point in mind: The larger the font the faster the screen fills up, leading to more scrolling for readers.[11]
- Keep the format simple: Omit paragraph indentations; allow lines of text to wrap naturally; insert a blank line below each paragraph; and aid readability with bulleted lists. If your e-mail lacks a bullet feature, create bullets using two hyphens (--).

Memo Format

Relatively brief internal reports may be written in interoffice memorandum—or memo—format. A commonly used memo format is shown in Figure 1.5.

The memo heading includes the guidewords To, From, Date, and Subject. The date may appear above the name of the recipient, if you prefer, without the word Date in front of it. Some organizations include other guidewords, such as cc, c, or copy.

{UbiQuiTous}

To: All Typing & Transcription Service Reps

From: Marilyn L. Hogue, Production Leader *mlh*

Date: July 16, 2019

Subject: Standard Memo Format

This report demonstrates memo format. (The word memo comes from the original name of this document: interoffice memorandum.) Please notice these features of memo format.

1. The standard heading consists of the captions *To*, *From*, *Date*, and *Subject*. Those captions may be arranged in different ways, but either *Date* or *To* should be the first item; and *Subject* should immediately precede the memo body (message). On a memo, the date may appear as shown or in *mm/dd/yy* or *mm/dd/yyyy* format.

2. The subject line must be a brief, meaningful summary of the memo's content.

3. The memo body has a blank line below the heading and below each paragraph.

4. Left and right margins should be at least one inch wide.

5. Numbering focuses the reader's attention on specific information, emphasizing items in top-to-bottom order. Numbered items also permit a reader to identify specific items for response. If a memo contains only one major point, do not number it.

6. The memo sender frequently writes her or his initials after the typed name to indicate approval of the message. Some writers sign or initial the memo at the end of the message. However, do not use a closing (such as Sincerely or Yours truly) at the end of a memo.

Figure 1.5 Report in memo format

Follow these guides as you prepare memo reports.

- Courtesy and professional titles (Mr., Mrs., Ms., Dr., and so on) are usually omitted in intracompany memos, but position titles (Vice President, Supervisor, and so on) are sometimes included. When beginning a new job in a large organization, showing your department affiliation is a good idea until others in the organization become acquainted with you. In any case, it is wise to check the organization's office manual or files to determine the preferences within that company.

- A memo template is a preformatted file containing place-holders and guides for completing a memo. Templates are designed to save users' time, and most word processing software offers a variety of memo templates. Online sources of memo templates include Microsoft Word Templates (www.wordtemplates.org/memo-word-templates/memorandum-template), Tidy Forms (www.tidyforms.com/business.html), and Vertex 42 (www.vertex42.com).

- Before using a template, find a design that conforms to your organization's standards. It may be necessary to adapt a template to your specifications and save it for future use.

Figures throughout the chapter illustrate form reports, e-mails, and memos.

Identifying Routine Reports

Illustrating every kind of simple report is impossible; but the models that follow illustrate the most common routine reports used in contemporary businesses: trip (travel) reports, production and performance reports, progress and status reports, and meeting reports.

Trip (Travel) Reports

Web conferencing and related technology has greatly reduced—but not eliminated—business travel in recent decades. Your career responsibilities may require that you travel away from your home base for a variety of reasons: to attend a convention or trade show, to observe activities at another work site, to interview a potential employee, to sell your company's products or services, and so on. The manager who authorizes your travel will be accountable for your time and expenses during the trip. Therefore, that manager needs information to evaluate whether the company benefits from your travel. The purpose of a trip report is to provide that information.

Generally, a trip report has two main parts: One part reports the benefits of the trip to your organization, and the other part reports your travel expenses. Trip benefits may be reported on a form or in e-mail or a memo and sent to the person who authorized your trip.

A report of trip benefits should be brief and factual—omitting personal reflections about the good, or bad, time you had. Provide complete, clear, well-organized information that will permit the reader to draw conclusions or take action. Appropriate content, organization, and writing style for reporting trip benefits are demonstrated in Figure 1.6.

Notice that the report uses a concise but complete subject line, headings that clearly identify topics, and a concrete request for response. (*Note*: The heading on page 2 showing the receivers name, page number, and date could be placed on separate lines at the left margin. This heading would be useful if the first and second pages became separated. Though still practical, this kind of heading is less important given the lower volume of paper documents in today's offices.) This report is organized by topics; but other patterns, such as chronological, could also be appropriate, depending on the content to be covered.

Traditionally, business travelers reported expenses to the company's accounting department on forms or in spreadsheets (Figure 1.7) and waited a week or two to be reimbursed for those expenses.

In addition, company travel policies usually require travelers to attach receipts for expenses over a specified amount, which could mean tracking a paper receipt for items listed on the form. Doing so is not a problem when the report, like the one shown in Figure 1.7, lists a single car trip. But when a person takes frequent, long trips, tracking airline, hotel, and restaurant receipts can become a hassle.

In many organizations, travel expense forms have been replaced by mobile apps and cloud software that create travel expense reports automatically as each expense is incurred before and during the trip. Thus, in the future if not currently, you will likely send your travel expense report using your mobile device as soon as your trip ends (or as you fly home). What about your receipts? Many receipts—airfare and hotel room, for instance—will be added automatically to your trip profile when you book the flight or reserve the room. For other expenses—such as the cost of a meal you host for clients—add it to your trip profile by snapping a picture of the paper receipt with your phone.

The following list identifies some providers of expense reporting software. View the listed sites to grasp the data gathering and analysis potential of these applications, besides how they streamline expense reporting.

PREMIER CONSTRUCTION

DATE: 04/13/2019

TO: Michael Dreyer

FROM: Noah Isaacs   *ni*

SUBJECT: Check on McNabb Project – 04/12/2019

As you requested, I went to Chesapeake yesterday to review the McNabb project and
determine why it has fallen behind schedule. Here is what I learned.

Construction Quality

All completed phases of the project meet our quality standards. Invoices and samples
of materials indicate that building materials meet the specifications set forth in our
RFPs. Files in the construction office contain reports from local building inspectors
showing that requirements of local codes have been met.

Construction Delays

Several factors contributed to construction delays during the past two months:

1. The supplier who was awarded the contract for plumbing supplies initially delivered substandard materials. The construction site manager, David Bowen, insisted
   on the quality specified in the contract. Those materials were delivered two weeks
   later.

2. Since our policy is to pay skilled-labor crews only when they are actually on the
   job, Bowen could not pay the plumbing crew while waiting for the materials. Consequently, that crew moved to another construction project.

3. Because of the high demand for and low supply of skilled-labor crews in the Chesapeake area, we lost another week while Bowen tried to hire a new plumbing crew.
   Naturally, some phases of construction could not be completed until the basic
   plumbing system was installed.

Requests

Bowen asks that he be authorized to pay skilled-labor crews for up to one week of
waiting time when delays are caused by shortages of materials. He acknowledges that
weather-related delays are normally considered an occupational hazard for which construction crews are not compensated. But in the Bay area's tight labor market, we risk
losing good crews if we refuse to pay them for other delays.

Additional Information

I have reminded Bowen that he must immediately report the failure of suppliers to
meet bid specifications. If he had reported the supplier's actions earlier, perhaps we
could have transferred plumbing materials from other projects or put pressure on the
supplier to fulfill the contract terms promptly.

Michael Dreyer   -2-   04/13/2019

I also asked Bowen to submit a monthly progress report detailing what has been completed, problems encountered, and any other information that will help us work with
him to meet project goals.

Request for Response

I promised Bowen that I'd give him an answer before April 30 about paying crews for
waiting time. Please let me know your decision.

Figure 1.6 Trip benefits report

PREMIER CONSTRUCTION Employee Travel Expenses Report		Any employees seeking reimbursement for authorized travel expenses, must complete this form. If you used your personal vehicle for transportation, enter mileage under Explanation. The 2017 reimbursement rate is 53.5 cents per mile. For other expense categories, attach a receipt for amounts over $40. Form 7808							
Name	Noah Isaacs	Trip Destination	Chesapeake city						
Position	Construction Projects Manager	Trip Purpose	Review McNabb Project						
Office Location	Baltimore	Trip Date(s)	April 12, 2019						
ID#	9355	Date Reported	April 30, 2019						

Date	Doc #	Explanation	Transport	Meals	Lodging	Entertain	Supplies	Misc	Total
04/12/19	7808	Personal vehicle							
		117.8 mi round trip							
		at $0.535/mi	$ 63.02	$ 27.64					$ 90.66
		Subtotals	$ 63.02	$ 27.64					$ 90.66
								Total	$ 90.66

Approved	Comments

Figure 1.7 Business travel expenses form (Form created in Microsoft Excel 365.)

Expense reporting software—

- Abacus (https://www.abacus.com)
- Concur (https://www.concur.com/en-us/travel-expense)
- ExpensAble (http://expensable.com)
- Nexonia (https://www.nexonia.com/nexonia-expenses)
- Zoho Expense (https://www.zoho.com/us/expense)

A worthwhile four-minute video on YouTube (Watch an expense report that writes itself!) demonstrates the Concur software and summarizes the concept of automatic travel expense reports. See it at https://youtube.com/watch?time_continue=13&v=7V12G-s_fd0

Production and Performance Reports

In most businesses, ensuring profitability is a day-to-day proposition of cutting costs and eliminating needless expenses. Therefore, productivity and efficiency levels are checked and compared periodically to monitor operations.

Most jobs require periodic reports about individual or team per-formance—production reports. Sales representatives, supervisors of manufacturing units, service technicians, and some office employ-ees—especially in small to medium-sized organizations—may be required to report production daily or weekly. In large organizations, other employees, such as insurance claims examiners, college profes-sors, librarians, or loan officers, may report on performance monthly, quarterly, or even annually. The closest that some employees come to preparing a production report occurs when they complete a self-evaluation before a formal performance appraisal. Even so, a self-eval-uation is a production report.

A performance report is important employee-to-manager feedback. The purpose of such a report is to let a manager or supervisor know whether individual employees or work units are meeting performance goals. The report usually identifies the following information.

- *Quantities and units of production.* Items include customers contacted, items manufactured, loans closed, claims processed during an identified period.
- *Comments about the production experience.* Comments might refer to difficulties encountered and how they were overcome or successes enjoyed.
- *Work plan or objectives for the next period.* If the report writer anticipates problems in carrying out the plan, the report should include those concerns.
- *Request for additional resources.* If the report writer sees a need for any additional resource, such as additional training, to meet the objectives, the report should request it.

These kinds of information help managers evaluate an individual employee's contributions to the organization's success. The report may tell the manager that all is well and no intervention is needed, or the report may provide evidence that potential or immediate problems require the manager's intervention or assistance.

A typical production report appears in Figure 1.8.

FAST TRACK DELIVERIES			
Sales Representative:	Powell Henderson	**Directions:** This form to be completed by all Fast Track **sales reps** each month. (Drivers who do not contact new clients should fill out form D-214 each month.) Turn in completed reports to the General Manager by the 5th for activity the previous month.	
Rep. Number:	301		
District:	7		
Month:	April		
Date Submitted:	05/01/19		
New Clients			
Prospects contacted	63		
New clients from those contacts	19		
Total pickups	123		
Total deliveries	51		
Total revenues, new clients		$21,010.50	
Current Clients			
Total pickups	326		
Total deliveries	215		
Total revenues, current clients		$65,325.75	
Total revenues for month			$86,336.25

Comments about clients

Twelve of the new clients used Package Xpress before that company closed. The clients compared Fast Track with our top two competitors before choosing us.

Plans for Next Month (Add pages if needed.)

The increasing volume of pickups and deliveries restricts the amount of time I can spend calling on prospective clients. I plan to hire a driver to handle most of the pickup and delivery work. I hope to have someone on the job by May 15.

I'll add one or two heavy-duty moving blankets to the equipment in my delivery vehicle. Thus, I will be prepared to carry fragile items.

--- Form D-966 ---

Figure 1.8 Production report form (Form created in Microsoft Word 365.)

Notice that the report form clearly identifies the kind of information the manager needs. If the company had not designed this form, the report could have been prepared in memo format as shown in Figure 1.9.

Although most production reports flow from subordinates to superiors, supervisors or managers may also send production reports to their subordinates. These reports are often summaries of the unit's production

---

FAST TRACK DELIVERIES

Date: May 1, 2019

To: Kira McKimson

From: Powell Henderson, Agent No. 301   *ph*

Subject: Sales and Delivery Activity, April 2019

By targeting new clients and providing prompt service to established clients, I have been able to increase revenues in my territory by approximately 33 percent in April. Here is a summary of my activity:

New Clients

Prospects contacted	63	
New clients from those contacts	19	
Total pickups	123	
Total deliveries	51	
Total revenues related to new clients		$21,010.50

Established Clients

Total pickups	326	
Total deliveries	215	
Total revenues from established clients		$65,325.75
Total Revenues		**$86,336.25**

Plans for May 2019

The increasing volume of pickups and deliveries restricts the amount of time I can spend calling on prospective clients. I plan to hire a driver to handle most of the pickup and delivery work. I hope to have someone on the job by May 15.

My goal for May is to add a minimum of 30 new clients and retain those currently using our services. With an assistant to handle the pickups and deliveries, I will have more time to contact potential clients and make follow-up calls on current users.

Figure 1.9 Monthly production report (employee to supervisor)

and may be sent to bolster the morale of a unit with evidence of its accomplishments. Since the main purpose of a supervisor-to-employee production report is to boost morale, an informal style and format is appropriate, as shown in Figure 1.10. *Note*: For sending a business report, a text message is suitable ONLY when the sender is certain that EVERY recipient does, in fact, receive and send texts and will not be offended by such informality. When in doubt, choose e-mail.

Thank you all for your diligent sales and service efforts. FT revenues for April were up 25% over March. You've done an A+ job of promoting same-day delivery and giving the service our clients rightfully expect. Please keep up the good work.

−Kira McKimson

Figure 1.10 Production report (supervisor to employees)

Progress (Status) Reports

A progress report is comparable to a production report in that it covers a set reporting period—usually weekly or monthly. However, a progress report is related to a major—usually one-time—project. In many organizations, no distinction is made between a progress report (advancement and change over time) and a status report (snapshot in time).[12]

Traditional Model

Progress reports, prepared by an individual or a project team, must include all information needed by upper-level managers to evaluate whether the project will be completed in keeping with the project management plan—most notably, on time and under budget.[13] Thus, a progress report contains information related to the project schedule and budget.

- *Current standing of the project and predicted completion dates* (entire project or significant parts of it). Basically, a progress report compares the planned schedule with actual timelines.[14] Some major projects involve contracts stipulating a penalty if the project is not completed as scheduled. In such instances, a progress report helps company managers prevent penalties resulting from failure to meet scheduled due dates.

    Usually, progress reports include information to support general statements about project status; specifically, (1) the main accomplishments since the previous report, (2) the difficulties encountered (if any) and how they were overcome, and (3) difficulties anticipated (if any).
- *Financial data related to accomplishments to date*, especially costs incurred up to the present. A progress report may compare actual costs with planned costs and may well include a forecast of the funds needed to complete the remaining work, as well as estimated total funds to complete the project.[15]

In recent years, the project management field has become more and more sophisticated. Today, project managers calculate a variety of metrics to keep projects on track and convey project status. One such statistic is the earned value of a project. The earned value shows how much of the budget and time should have been spent, considering the amount of work done so far.[16] *Note*: An illustration of earned value is beyond the scope of this book. For treatment of project evaluation methods, see books by Larson and Gray,[17] Scott,[18] and Verzuh.[19]

Progress reports must be written in a style, structure, and format that permit a manager to learn quickly what is happening on a project for which that manager is accountable. Therefore, the reports often include bullet points and visuals—such as graphs, photos, and tables—along with plain text. Study the content and style of the progress report in Figure 1.11, which includes a bulleted list and a table.

PPP Model

PPP is a management practice for daily, weekly, or monthly progress reporting. The three Ps stand for progress, plans, and problems; and the reporting method is remarkably straightforward. Each status report consists of the writer's name, the start and end dates of the reporting period, and the three lists shown in Figure 1.12.[20]

City Central Hospital

DATE: May 31, 2019

TO: Frederick Cox, VP, Medical Affairs

FROM: Chao-chen Yang, Operations Manager   *ccy*

SUBJECT: Progress on Improving Efficiency of Emergency Room Procedures

We are well on the road to improving the efficiency of emergency room procedures here at City Central Hospital.

Tasks Completed

During the past three months we have established the foundation for improving procedures in the emergency room. Specifically, we have:

- Held meetings with key members of the emergency room staff to inform them of our plans to study our current operations with a goal of reducing patients' wait time.

- Contracted with LeQuire and Associates to study our emergency room procedures and apply current operations and supply chain theory to an analysis of our ER operations.

- Enabled researchers from LeQuire and Associates to observe emergency room procedures and access hospital records related to patient processing time.

- Received a written report from LeQuire and Associates, along with an oral briefing of the findings and recommendations. A major finding was that 85% of the problems encountered in moving patients through the ER were related to administrative bottlenecks, not to competencies of doctors and nurses.

- Obtained budget approval for five Patient Flow Coordinators (PFCs) and started recruiting for those positions.

Recommendations for Improving ER Efficiency

LeQuire made two major recommendations:

- Assign each incoming patient to a PFC immediately upon the patient's entering the ER facility. The PFCs will track patients from start to finish through admission, diagnosis, and treatment. This tracking system should ensure that patients are moved through the system more rapidly and also reassure patients that they have not been forgotten.

- Require medical personnel to use checklists for procedures (much like those used by airline pilots before they start a jetliner's engines) to ensure that all protocols are followed. The discipline and efficiency of using such a checklist should improve the speed and quality of ER services.

Figure 1.11 Traditional progress report

Frederick Cox
Page 2
May 31, 2019

Problems Encountered

Although ER personnel generally favored employing Patient Flow Coordinators, some objected to completing the checklist. However, LeQuire associates were able to demonstrate the advantages of using a checklist to speed up the diagnosis and treatment process. ER personnel are now on board with that recommended change in operations.

Target Dates for Remainder of Project

We plan to have our patient flow coordination plan fully operational on July 1, the beginning of the next fiscal year.

That timing will enable us to do an effective cost-benefit analysis after one year of operation. Specific targets are:

June   15   Complete hiring of Patient Flow Coordinators

June   20   Complete training of PFCs

June   21-25   Conduct trial run of new flow system, including use of checklists by medical personnel

June   25-29   Identify and implement any changes resulting from trial run

June   30   Have all procedures in place and personnel confident about their use

Financial Information

Total Project Budget $500,000
Planned Value (budgeted to date) $375,000
Actual Cost (expenditures to date).................................... $360,000
Earned Value (project is 80% complete) $400,000
Schedule Variance (EV-PV) .... $ 25,000
Cost Variance (EV-AC) .... $ 40,000

Since both variance amounts are positive numbers, these financials indicate the project is **ahead of schedule** and **under budget**.

Beginning with five PFCs will enable us to maintain a flexible schedule that will get us through the ebbs and flows of ER traffic. The ER will be staffed always by a minimum of two PFCs; during the busiest times, it will be staffed by five. That number will be reviewed after three months to decide whether five PFCs are enough to handle the heaviest loads. If needed, we will request budget approval to increase the number.

Figure 1.11 (Continued)

Users of the technique at well-known organizations, such as Apple, eBay, Facebook, and Skype, like PPP because the informal reports can be written and read quickly, and virtually every word conveys useful and relevant information.[21] PPP reports may be completed in progress reporting software, such as KeyedIn® (https://keyedin.com), Supdate (http://supdate.com), and Working On (https://workingon.co) or full-scale project management

Progress Report Content Using PPP Reporting Method	
Progress	**Examples**
Each report writer lists three to five achievements since previous report.	• Set production schedules for four incoming titles. • Reviewed author's CE corrections for Bel96313. • Completed QC spot checks on four CEs' work. • Copyedited Ch01 of Dav74191 for author approval. • Participated in supervisory management webinar (Taking the Lead: 5 Things All Supervisors Need to Know).
Plans	**Examples**
Each employee also lists three to five goals for the next reporting period.	• Copyedit sample chapter of Alb63080 for author approval. • Make author's corrections for Bel96313 and mark CE for typesetter. • Participate in supervisory management webinar (The Top 10 Mistakes Managers Make and How to Avoid Them). • Lead meeting of CE Team to brainstorm how we can help shorten production cycle by 25% within nine months.
Problems	**Examples**
Additionally, each person lists three to five challenges or problems, such as tasks that cannot be finished without help from someone else.	• Parts of text for DAV74191 not in TNR-12, double-spaced, causing work to slow down. Normal CE output is 12 to 15 pages per hour, depending on content. Output on DAV74191 was 10 pages per hour. Need to (1) emphasize font consistency in instructions for authors and editors and (2) skim incoming text for font consistency before copyedit begins. • Problem of distracting sounds that I reported two weeks ago has been eliminated. The entire CE Team joined the Noisli website, a white noise generator, and use it several hours each day. • Symptoms of Carpal Tunnel Syndrome suggest installing a keyboard tray for my use.

Figure 1.12 Contents of a progress report using the PPP method

software, such as Asana (https://asana.com), Basecamp (https://basecamp.com), and Wrike (https://wrike.com), all of which offer special efficiency features.

In some organizations, PPP reports are "aggregated and delivered up the management chain, all the way up to executive board, with bits being added and removed to tailor the message for the target audience."[22] The informality of PPP reports suggests using plain-text e-mail as the format and delivery method. However, in some organizations, the PPP reports have such importance and value that individuals prepare the reports in HTML (web page format), using color, emphasis techniques, and so on.[23] Some PPP users cite it as a productivity booster and facilitator of all management functions (planning, organizing, staffing, coordinating, and controlling) in addition to its use for status reports.[24]

Generally, progress reports are sent by employees to their managers. However, PPP reports are often sent by team members to the team (who appreciate knowing what their co-workers are doing) and by the CEO to the board of directors, investors, and advisors.[25] By sending a monthly PPP report to stakeholders (persons with an interest or concern in your organization[26]) and other contacts outside your company, you may get innovative solutions to your reported problems (without asking for them).[27] As you view Figure 1.13, imagine that the report's sender or receiver, knowing your interest in City Central Hospital, forwarded it to you.

When writing PPP reports, some businesspeople put brevity above all other considerations and, thus, produce shoddy output. Following these guides will help you avoid common missteps.[28]

- As a rule, list three to five items in each category. Occasionally, five to seven items may seem more appropriate, such as when you aggregate several reports into one. To stay within seven items when aggregating, you may include only the most significant items reported to you; or you may combine two or more closely related items.
- State each item concisely but make every item informative. To do so: Instead of writing complete sentences, use fragments, or abbreviated sentences, which resemble newspaper headlines. (*Note*: Use this technique only if English is the native language of the person reading your reports.[29])

  Abbreviated sentences contain only words that impart meaning, while omitting filler words, such as the following.
  articles (a, an, and the)
  the verb be
  possessive adjectives (her, his, my, our, and your) before
      a noun
  personal pronouns (I, you, he, she, it, we, they)

prepositions (with, at, from, into, during, including, until, against, among, and throughout).[30] *Note*: The English language contains about 150 prepositions. The preceding list shows, in frequency order, the most-used prepositions, identified in a study by TalkEnglish.com.[31]

- Use parallel grammatical structure in each list. Starting each item with an action verb, as shown in Figure 1.13, is effective.
- Remember to write from your reader's viewpoint, not yours. Review your report, pretending you are that person. Should you define any technical terms or provide any background information?
- For each list, use a bold heading above it and use bullets.
- At the top of your report, place identifying information: your name, the period covered by the report, and any other information that has become standard in your organization. At the end, summarize.

Meeting Reports

Much of an organization's business is conducted in meetings—some face-to-face meetings and many virtual meetings. These sessions may range from the meeting of a project team, a standing committee, or an ad hoc committee within a company to a major gathering of professional or trade association members. In all cases, the person who organizes and leads, or chairs, the meeting is responsible for informing participants—and often company managers—of upcoming meeting activities and results of the meetings. The most common tools for communicating such information are the meeting agenda and meeting minutes, or summary.

Meeting Agenda

An agenda is simply a list of events to occur during a meeting. Clear, well-planned agendas make for productive meetings that participants

City Central Hospital

June 30, 2019

To: Frederick Cox

From: Chao-chen Yang *ccy*

Quarterly Progress Report (ER Project) for April-June 2019

Progress

- Met with ER staff three times to explain objective of reducing patients' wait time and the plans for doing so.

- Hired LeQuire and Associates to study ER procedures and recommend improvements based on operations and supply chain theory.

- Obtained authorization for LeQuire researchers to observe ER procedures and access hospital records of patient processing time.

- Received LeQuire's written and oral reports and began implementing recommendations, starting with setting up a new position, Patient Flow Coordinator (PFC), to track patients from admission to the end of treatment.

- Obtained budget approval for five PFCs and started recruiting for those positions.

Plans

- Complete hiring of Patient Flow Coordinators by July 15 and complete training them by July 20.

- Conduct trial run of the new flow system on July 21 to 25.

- Identify and implement any changes noted during the trial run on July 25 to 29.

- Add all new procedures to our online Hospital Policy & Procedures Manual by July 30.

Problems

- Some ER personnel objected initially to completing a MediPro checklist for each incoming patient but are now on board after LeQuire's demo of the checklist.

- One member of hospital administration and one member of the medical team are needed to monitor the trial run with me and then help identify necessary changes.

- Publishing new procedures in Manual may not be enough. To help ensure their use, will you call a 20-minute meeting for all stakeholders on Tuesday, July 30, at 3 or 3:30. I'll give a 5-minute presentation, followed by Q and A and five minutes for open discussion.

Figure 1.13 Progress report using PPP

like to attend. One blogger noted, "It does not matter if it is a weekly team meeting, a board meeting, a sales meeting, an annual review, a marketing meeting, annual stockholders meeting or whatever meeting, having an agenda is a must."[32] Naturally it does not matter if it is a face-to-face or virtual meeting. An agenda clearly limits what will be discussed during the meeting, and it helps to maintain focus and keep participants involved.

Agenda Structure

A complete agenda includes the name of the person or agency calling the meeting and the date, time, and location of the meeting. In addition, a good agenda indicates who should attend and who should be prepared to discuss certain items listed for discussion. Also, an effective meeting agenda includes the start and end time for each item of business on it.[33] Obviously, a meeting agenda includes a schedule of business to be conducted. The schedule of business is often structured as follows:

- *Call to order.* The chairperson or leader announces that the meeting has begun. This announcement may be only two or three words to end any hubbub and bring participants to attention.
- *Review of events in the previous meeting.* In a board or professional association meeting, this review usually involves formally correcting and approving the minutes (summary) of the previous meeting. In a business team or department meeting, accomplishments of the previous session are reviewed.
- *Reports of identified meeting participants.* In organizations that have standing committees or subcommittees, a representative of each one orally reports highlights of the committee's work. Then a representative of each special committee or subcommittee also reports.

  Business departments and teams that meet monthly often have a member serve as liaison with other parts of the organization, such as human resources, information technology (IT), legal affairs, and social media optimization (SMO). In addition, many organizations keep close ties with national watchdog agencies, such as Consumer Product Safety Commission (CPSC), Environmental Protection Agency (EPA), Federal Communication Commission (FCC), and Occupational Safety and Health Administration (OSHA), and their local equivalents. Each liaison officer reports any information that may affect the department's or team's work.

- *Unfinished business.* Here the agenda includes a detailed list of topics discussed previously but allocated to the next meeting for resolution. If done correctly, the previous meeting ended with action items, or agreed-upon assignments. Each specific assignment (action and the person responsible) appears on the meeting agenda. Then individuals with assigned action items report each item's status.

- *New business.* This section of the agenda contains a list of topics not discussed previously. The agenda indicates who will introduce each narrow, specific topic.

- *Summary and review.* During this part of the meeting, the leader summarizes the decisions reached during the meeting and reviews action items. He or she names each task assigned and the person responsible for it.

- *Announcements and comment.* This phase of the meeting involves sharing important company news that is unrelated to discussion topics. (Routine announcements are better sent by e-mail.) While some business leaders open meetings with announcements and recognitions,[34] others prefer placing announcements last on the agenda so as not to distract participants from the meeting's main purpose. This time is also for participants to bring up information or concerns about the group process (how an organization's members work together to get things done). These comments about member interactions are also called good of the order.

- *Adjournment.* The meeting chair, or leader, ensures that all announcements and comments have been made before stating that the meeting is adjourned, or ended.

Some meetings may not require all elements listed, and some may include additional items, such as an open period for exchanging ideas among the participants.[35] In fact, meetings can be divided into two distinct categories: formal and informal. Formal meetings have a fixed structure and use definite rules, including the rules of debate. (See information about Robert's Rules of Order later in this chapter). Examples of formal meetings include board meetings, committee meetings, caucus meetings, council meetings, legislatures, and stock-holders' meetings.[36]

Most meetings in a work setting do not fit the foregoing definition. Work meetings are viewed as informal meetings because they are apt to vary in structure and follow rules that are relatively lax.[37]

In any case, an effective agenda includes everything that will enable participants to come to the meeting prepared to conduct business effi-ciently. As you view the agenda in Figures 1.14 and 1.15, notice features that will help participants prepare for these meetings.

Agenda Planning

A truly useful meeting agenda involves careful planning. Start planning early, beginning with your purpose and goal(s) for the meeting. What is the point of bringing people together? What do you expect to accomplish

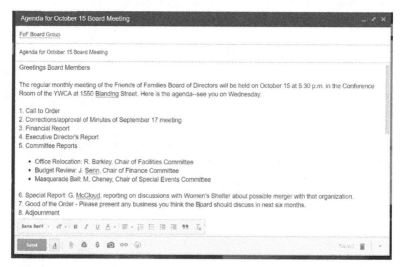

Figure 1.14 Agenda for a formal meeting

Note: Participants in this formal meeting do not work for the same employer, and the group is sizable. Therefore, the informal medium of e-mail seems the most effective way to distribute the meeting agenda.

Agenda		
"Catch the Drift" Film Production Meeting		
When:	July 16, 2019, from 11 a.m. to 1:30 p.m.	
Where:	Conference Room D	
Purposes:	• Review and complete the film script • Plan ways to raise funds for this film • Decide the pre-production timeline	
Attendees:	Jason David, Producer Juanita Janick, Writer-Director Lok Chén - Creative Director Zaha Ahmad - Development Director	
Schedule:	11:00 to 11:15	Check-in and General Updates – Lok Chén
	11:15 to 11:45	Script Review and Recent Changes – Juanita Janick
	11:45 to 1:00	Fundraising Updates – Zaha Ahmad
	1:00 to 1:15	Pre-Production Timeline – Jason David
	1:15 to 1:30	Comments and Announcements – All Participants
Roles:	• Take notes and prepare meeting summary - **Jason David** • Keep meeting on point and on schedule - **Lok Chén**	

Figure 1.15 Agenda for an informal meeting (Form created in Microsoft Word 365.)

Note: The few participants at this informal meeting do work together closely in the same organization. Thus, a printed agenda can be delivered easily. Also, each person can use the space at the bottom of the page to jot ideas that come to mind before the meeting.

by meeting? Without a specific purpose and clear-cut goals, you cannot be sure a meeting is needed and you cannot expect to use participants' time wisely. So, do not proceed without knowing precisely why you are calling a meeting. Once you have identified your purpose and goal(s), write them down.

Then follow these guides to develop an agenda that will propel and control your meeting.[38]

- *Narrow the meeting's focus as much as possible.* Carefully describe (in writing) each topic that requires discussion. Avoid adding sideline topics to the list.
- *Based on the meeting's purpose, make these critical decisions:*
  - o *Who should participate in the meeting?* Do not invite people who have little or nothing to do with the meeting topics. Do invite everyone who will be responsible for carrying out the decisions and plans made in the meeting.
  - o *When should the meeting be held?* Give all participants adequate lead time to prepare for the meeting, including time to think about and recommend agenda items.

    Of course, you will select a day and time when all or most of the participants are available to attend a meeting. If you are planning a web conference, your meeting software—such as Cisco WebEx (https://webex.com), GoToMeeting (www.gotomeeting.com), or Meeting-King (http://meetingking.com)—has a built-in calendar app you can use to set a meeting time. Basically, the app accesses all participants' calendars and produces for you a list of times when most, if not all, participants are available. If you are planning a face-to-face meeting, a shared calendar app, such as Calendly (https://calendly.com), Clara (https://claralabs.com), or Doodle (http://doodle.com), will enable you to choose an appropriate meeting time.

    In recent studies, researchers concluded that 3 p.m. on Tuesday (in the United States) is a good time for both maximum attendance and optimum performance. If you are planning a virtual meeting involving participants outside the United States, a world map of time zones (www.worldtimezone.com) may be helpful.

In addition, rely on the experience of other meeting leaders in your organization.

o *How long should the meeting continue?* Make each meeting as long as it must be and as short as it can be—say, 60 to 90 minutes at most. On the agenda sent to participants in advance, show a time limit for the whole meeting and for each agenda item. In the meeting, if an item demands more time than you allocated for it, place that item on a list to be treated as unfinished business at a later meeting.

o *Where should the group meet?* If all participants work in the same location, then schedule a face-to-face meeting on the premises. If participants are scattered around the city, country, or world, consider the costs of travel (dollars plus lost time) versus an online meeting (web conference). In general, businesspeople today travel much less frequently than they did just 10 years ago.

Face-to-face meetings are required in at least three situations: (1) meeting content is confidential or highly sensitive; (2) most participants are unfamiliar with virtual meeting technology or unsupportive of it; or (3) no bond exists among participants going into a persuasive or problem-solving meeting. While meeting physically is essential for building relationships among participants, most meetings are held to complete tasks or make decisions or plans that do not require participant bonding.

• *Add only those agenda items that relate to your purpose and goals.* Also, make sure each item is relevant to all participants. If not, consider holding two or more separate meetings. Another possibility: Plan the agenda so that certain participants attend for only the topic(s) relevant to them. Make keeping participants engaged and enthusiastic a high priority.

- *Provide any supporting materials participants need to study before the meeting.* Identify the materials, such as an advertisement or a brochure, PDF document, press release, or web link, on the agenda. If the materials apply to the whole meeting, list them near the top, labeled Preparation. Otherwise, identify the materials with the business item(s) to which they do apply.
- *Include your contact information* for participants who may have questions about the agenda.

Having used the agenda to prepare everyone involved, use it throughout your meeting, too. Watch the times allocated for agenda items and stay within those limits—even when someone else oversees an agenda item. Thus, you can keep your meeting moving and the participants engaged. As noted earlier, ensure that uncompleted discussions will appear as unfinished business on the next meeting's agenda. In a web conference, use software features to transfer items from your current agenda to the new one. In a face-to-face meeting, jot a note on your phone or a notepad or ask the person taking notes to also keep a list of unfinished items.

To further enhance your skills as a meeting leader, refer to one or more of these publications: blogs by Bryant,[39] McCarthy,[40] and McNamara[41] and books by Harvard Business Review,[42] Herold,[43] and Williams.[44]

Meeting Minutes or Summary

To ensure accurate records of its accomplishments, every group that conducts meetings should identify someone to take notes during the meeting and summarize the meeting afterwards. That person's task is to take notes during the group's deliberations and provide minutes, a written record of the meeting outcomes. The minutes are distributed to meeting participants and other persons who have an interest in those proceedings.

In very formal meetings—a corporation's board of directors or a city's governing council, for instance—the recorder is typically not a member of the group but a highly skilled note taker hired to prepare a permanent record of each meeting. In contrast, in many formal and informal meetings the note taker, or recorder, is a member of the group appointed or elected to the role.

Sometimes in web conferences, the meeting leader may record notes and, with the aid of software features, distribute a summary at the end of the meeting.

Minutes, the official record of a meeting, are summaries of actions taken, not verbatim transcripts of the deliberations. They range from a one-page summary for a team meeting to book form for a convention or annual board meeting. Minutes are vital for several reasons, shown in Figure 1.16.[45]

Meeting minutes vary depending upon the type of organization holding the meeting. The minutes for a board of trustees meeting, a committee meeting, and a team meeting will differ markedly in content, writing style, and format. Meeting minutes will fall into one of three categories.[46]

- *Action*—minutes omit discussion and capture the decisions made and actions taken and to be taken. Action minutes are a general requirement of board, council, and hearing meetings. Work groups also often use action minutes.
- *Discussion*—includes decisions and actions and a summary of the discussion that led to them. Discussion is the most-used

5 Reasons for Meeting Minutes
To aid collective memory
Minutes emphasize actions taken, decisions made, and tasks assigned. Thus, all meeting participants by referring to the minutes can refresh their memory of proceedings—especially of tasks assigned to them and the due dates.
To inform non-attending members
When someone invited to a meeting cannot attend, the minutes can provide missing information until the next meeting.
To inform non-participating stakeholders
Anyone who will eventually implement the decisions made can benefit by getting the information sooner rather than later.
To conform to an organizations' by-laws
Some associations from their inception have rules for the content, writing style, and format of minutes—even the storage media to be used to preserve old records.
To comply with legal requirements
In some instances, local bylaws require meeting minutes for certain types of organizations, such as public-school boards and parent-teacher associations. Most states require careful activity records for S corporations and C corporations. Each time a corporation's board of directors meets, for example, the meeting minutes should be filed as proof of compliance with Internal Revenue Service (IRS) regulations if needed.
Note: An S corporation of 100 shareholders or fewer has the benefit of incorporation but is taxed as a partnership. In a C corporation, profits pass to the owners and are taxed at the individual level.

Figure 1.16 Purposes of meeting minutes

kind of minutes, perhaps because groups want to trace their decision-making process and identify areas of expertise among individual members.

- *Verbatim*—word-for-word transcript of who said what during a meeting. Verbatim minutes are used when required by law and in public hearings and congressional meetings. Otherwise, a verbatim transcript is practically never used.

Minutes narrate a meeting's substance accurately, clearly, and concisely. The language of minutes reflects the meeting itself: A formal meeting calls for a formal writing style, and informal language is appropriate for an informal meeting.[47]

Minutes of a formal meeting usually include the following data:

- Identification of group
- Type of meeting (regular, monthly, quarterly, special, or emergency)
- Location, date, and time of meeting
- Identification of people in attendance and the person presiding
- Identification of absentees along with reasons for the absences and whether the absence was excused or unexcused
- Reference to minutes of previous meeting: accepted as presented or amended and then accepted
- Reports of action on matters previously presented to the group (unfinished business)
- Reports of action on matters currently presented to the group (new business)
- Identity of any materials distributed in the meeting, along with copies or a link.
- Reports of good-of-the-order information
- Place and time of next meeting if known
- Time of adjournment
- Identification of person who prepared the minutes

Formats for formal meeting minutes vary among organizations, but the format should enable each reader to focus easily on any item that may be of special interest to that person. The report in Figure 1.17 summarizes a professional association's meeting.

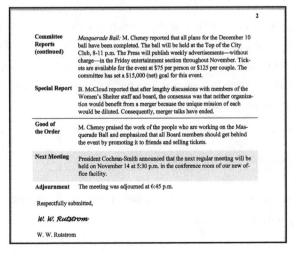

Figure 1.17 Minutes for a formal meeting (Form created in Microsoft Word 365.)

Minutes of an informal meeting should include the following information.[48] To distinguish achievements, decisions, and action items, examples are given.

- Purpose of the meeting and what it was about
- Where and when the meeting was held
- List of the attendees (first and last names). If someone invited did not attend and decisions cannot be made without him or her, this information should be included in the minutes.
- What was achieved during the meeting. Examples:

> Team reviewed home page image options (decided to order 4 images).
> Team discussed how many project management articles to include on website; settled on 5.

- Decisions made at the meeting. Examples:

> Team decided to omit budget template on PM Office website.
> Team decided not to add web sources for PM articles to the site.

- All action items agreed upon. An action item is a discrete task that must be accomplished, usually by a single individual or a small team or group. The meeting summary should include the action itself, who it was assigned to, and the due date for completion. Examples:

| Cancel photographer | ErvSwillinger | 10/25/2019 |
| Forward PMI articles to Lyle Knepper | Carrie Pacino | 11/05/2019 |

Also, any relay items; that is, action items that are expected to arise from the original one, should be included in the meeting minutes.

- The date, time, and location of a follow-up meeting if one was announced.

The formats for informal meeting minutes also vary among organizations. However, many organizations use a form designed by someone in the company. For web conferences, format of the meeting summary usually is determined by template options in the web conference software. The form in Figure 1.18 contains a work team's meeting summary.[49]

The use of a sans serif font in Figure 1.18 suggests that this meeting summary was posted on the team's website, rather than printed.

Team Meeting Summary	Project Name:	PMO Website	
	Date:	Thursday, May 23, 2019	
	Time:	3 to 3:30 p.m.	
Participants:	Dave Fitzpatrick, Pote Jantara, Anu Shakar		
Missing Team Member:	Emma Jewell		

Summary of 5/23 Agenda Items

1. Team reviewed home page image options and will buy 2 photos instead of taking them ourselves.
2. Team reviewed "Project Management Office Metrics" section on home page and a metrics data PDF.
3. Team discussed project management articles and will post fewer than originally thought.
4. Team studied Dave's meeting agenda example for the site and gave him feedback.
5. Team discussed status of the following Action Items from the 5/16 meeting:
   - Pote will send Dave links to helpful project management websites for adding to Resources tab.
   - Pote will send Dave samples for "FTP Planning" and "Risk Matrix."
   - Dave will request additional Budget templates from Sarah.
   - Anu will request final approval of Project Management Menu of Services document from Sarah.
   - Emma will forward PMI articles we can publish on our site to Dave.

Decisions Made:	1. Team decided to buy 2 stock photos from Snapstock for home page.
	2. Team decided not to include Budget template on PMO website.
	3. Team decided to limit PM articles on the website to 4 at a time.
	4. Team decided that additional website sources for PM articles are unnecessary.
	5. Team decided to update the "Active PMO Projects" worksheet quarterly (JAN, APR, JUL, OCT).
Issues Identified:	None

Action Items

#	Item	Assigned To	Due Date
1	Request final approval of PM Menu of Services document from Sarah.	Anu Shakar	06/04/19
2	Get Sarah's final approval on 2 images from Snapstock.	Anu Shakar	06/04/19
3	Forward PMI articles to Dave.	Emma Jewell	06/04/19
4	Send RFP/RFI process to Dave.	Pote Jantara	06/04/19
5	Forward Snapstock photos to Anu.	Dave Fitzpatrick	05/28/19
6	Edit Metrics Data PDF and "PMO Metrics" section on home page	Dave Fitzpatrick	06/04/19
7	Cancel photo shoot	Dave Fitzpatrick	05/28/19

Figure 1.18 Minutes for an informal meeting (Form created in Microsoft Word 365.)

Notice that the list of action items for this meeting can be lightly edited then copied into the next meeting's agenda. Also notice that the number of action items and decisions is roughly equal to the number of agenda items—indicating a productive meeting. A meeting summary showing, say, nine agenda items and only a couple decisions and two or three action items indicates an unproductive meeting. Those same discussion items will be discussed again at the next meeting or dropped altogether—resulting in wasted time either way. Whenever you lead a meeting, aim for at least one action item for each item on your agenda.

The following guides will help you record, report, and distribute meeting minutes.[50] Guides to use before, during, and after the meeting are also useful for coaching anyone who records minutes in the meetings you lead.

Before the meeting:

- *Study the meeting agenda* and make sure you understand everything on it. Also review related documents, such as previous meeting minutes.
  - o Use the agenda as an outline for taking notes. If you will use a laptop, phone, or tablet, type your notes into the agenda. If you will use pen and paper, print the agenda after inserting ample space between agenda items.
  - o Some expert note takers recommend taking minutes in Agreedo (https://agreedo.com), Evernote (https://ever-note.com), OneNote Online (https://onenote.com/hrd), or Textpad (https://.textpad.com/index.html). Again, scan or type the agenda into the note taking software.
  - o From the agenda, make a glossary of names (people, products, competitors, and so on) you are likely to encounter in the meeting.
  - o Include in the glossary abbreviations and acronyms for words and phrases that will likely occur often, such as business to consumer (B2C), management (mgmt), marketing (mktg), productivity (prod or prod-y),

project management (PM), public relations (PR) and value added tax (VAT). *Note:* To find lists of standard abbreviations and acronyms in business and many other fields, go to the Abbreviations website (www.abbreviations.com).[51] For each participant on the agenda, to avoid duplicates, include three—not two—initials in your glossary.

o Study minutes of the past several meetings before taking a meeting cold (recording meeting notes for the first time or for someone else). Notice the writing style, especially the level of formality, and the format of the minutes.

• *Know when to recommend hiring a professional note taker.* Even if you have been a good, reliable note taker for a group, consider bringing in a professional note taker in the following situations.

o The meeting will be unusually complex.

  1. Heated argument seems inevitable.
  2. Participants are senior members of the organization.
  3. Discussion will attack the culture—the core—of the organization.
  4. A decision must be made very quickly.
  5. The need for confidentiality is critical.

o You need to fully participate in the meeting, including controversial topics.

o Minutes must be distributed within 24 hours or the same day.

  You may experience other circumstances that call for bringing in a professional note taker. A list of commendable note taking services includes:

• Atchison & Denman (http://stenographers.com/minute-taking)

• GlobalLingo (www.global-lingo.com/minute-taking-services)

• HMSS (http://hmss.co.za)

- Minutes Solutions (https://minutessolutions.com)
- Quorum Secretarial Services (www.minutetakers.co.za)
- Ubiqus (https://ubiqus.com).

- *Arrive at the meeting early* so you have time to set up properly.
  o Though you plan to record notes on a laptop or tablet, take a paper tablet and a couple pens as back up.
  o If you will be using your phone and a voice recorder app to capture the entire meeting (for filling in gaps in your notes), turn the phone to airplane mode to prevent interruptions during the meeting. In addition, be sure the meeting leader approves a voice recording and that all participants know they are being recorded.

- *Check off participants' names as they arrive.* If the group is large, take a checklist of everyone invited. Save time during the meeting by checking names as participants arrive. Also note (with an x) which members do not attend. Update the list if someone arrives after the meeting begins.
  o Some note takers recommend circulating an attendance list that participants checkmark or initial. Such a list works well if you already know meeting participants by name—and the list, in fact, reaches all participants.
  o If you do not know everyone at the meeting, ask to ensure that names are recorded correctly.
  o Again, if someone invited did not attend and decisions cannot be made without her or him, include this information in the minutes.
  o In formal meetings, ensure there is a quorum (smallest number of the regular participants who must be present for the group to make decisions validly). A quorum is normally one-half of the regular participants plus one.

- *For formal meetings, become familiar with Robert's Rules of Order.* Robert's Rules of Order is a standard for running meetings and making decisions as a group. It is a widely used reference for meeting procedure and business rules in countries where English is the dominant language. Robert's Rules of Order is intended to answer, as nearly as possible, any question of parliamentary procedure that may come up. (Do not be misled by the word parliamentary, which refers to governmental groups. The reference is meant for use in ordinary groups rather than legislative bodies.[52]) The latest edition of the reference is a paperback titled *Robert's Rules of Order Newly Revised in Brief,* 2nd edition.[53] A very basic introduction to Robert's Rules of Order is available online.[54]

During the meeting:

- *Record decisions, achievements, and action items the instant they occur.* Making a note promptly is the best way to ensure accurate notes—and accurate minutes.
- *Clarify decisions in the meeting.* Before the leader moves on to a new agenda item, make sure a clear decision has been made and recorded (except when an item will be carried over to the next meeting). Ask for clarification in these situations, too.
  - Many suggestions are made about the action to take
  - Discussion jumps from topic to topic without a conclusion
  - Long discussion ends with no apparent conclusion
  - You participate in the meeting and forget to take notes
- *Maintain neutrality in controversies.* To be effective in the note taker role, you must be viewed as objective, or neutral, by other participants. In addition, when you disagree with an item, guard against omitting it from your notes.
- *Listen and mentally rephrase and summarize when not recording notes.* Doing so can save you time when turning your notes into minutes. Also, this practice keeps you engaged throughout the meeting.

After the meeting:

- *Clear up any remaining questions immediately after the meeting.* If you are still unsure about names or terms, speak briefly with the meeting leader or other representative. *Note*: Seek answers to your questions about achievements, decisions, and action items during the meeting before the next agenda item comes up.
- *Edit your meeting notes for clarity.* Soon after the meeting refer to your notes and draft the report. To avoid omitting important details, allow your first draft to be too wordy. Then revise and edit to ensure conciseness and objectivity.
  - When editing, strike most adjectives (describing words) to make your writing more objective. Although members of a committee comment about the superior quality of a subcommittee's work, say, the minutes should report only the facts presented by the subcommittee and the action taken by the full group. Unless the group passes an official resolution that includes descriptive words (such as brilliant, outstanding, superb; or faulty, inefficient, ineffective), the recorder should avoid descriptive adjectives. Rather than reflecting the group's opinion, those terms may represent only the recorder's interpretation of what occurred.
  - Also, strike most pronouns (words that substitute for the name of a person or group, such as he, her, his, I, it, me, our, she, someone, them, they, we, who, you, and yours). Repeating the person's or group's name will add clarity to your writing.
  - For a formal meeting, refer to participants by last name, not first name or nickname. For small, informal meetings, show each person's first and last name in the list of participants; thereafter, the first name alone is acceptable.

o If your notes contain negative wording, edit the text to use positive words. Though your notes may say "a heated argument," change it to "a lively discussion."

o For clarity, express each action item as a full sentence, not a sketchy note. Examples follow.

> Vague note: "Cygnus RFP."
>
> Clear sentence: "Draft a request for proposal (RFP) to Cygnus Applied Research, Inc."

- *Use the same format for each meeting of a group.* In addition, make information easy to find by using bold headings, bullet points, and numbered lists. Consider adopting or adapting a minutes template in your word processing software, such as the Formal meeting template or Informal meeting template in Microsoft Word. Using a template saves time and ensures a consistent format.

- *Enlist someone as an editor* once you have drafted, revised, and edited the minutes. This person does not have to be a participant. Ask the editor to point out anything confusing or incomplete and any grammar, punctuation, and usage errors, along with errors in the spelling of names.

- *Have the meeting leader review, revise if necessary, and approve the minutes* before distributing them to participants. For formal meetings, getting the chairperson's approval is standard practice. For some informal meetings, this approval may not be required.

- *Distribute your minutes promptly*—within 24 to 48 hours. The meeting and your notes will still be fresh in your mind. In addition, participants with action items to pursue will receive an early reminder of that responsibility.

- *For distributing meeting minutes, use the best medium available to you.* A wiki can be an ideal place to store minutes, where all participants can see them, plus offer additional input after the meeting has ended.

  o If your organization uses web conference software, you can use its built-in e-mail to send the minutes.

- o If you and all participants use Google Docs or another collaboration app, simply share the minutes with the group that way.
- o If your organization uses a cloud-based member management system, you can publish the minutes as a web page and provide access only to the meeting participants and selected stakeholders. Examples of cloud-based member management systems include the following.
  - GrowthZone (http://unbouncepages.com/growthzone-gdm)
  - Member365 (https://member365.com/membership-trial)
  - MemberClicks (www.memberclicks.com)
  - MindBody (https://www.mindbodyonline.com/overview)
  - NeonCRM (https://www.neoncrm.com)
  - Wild Apricot (https://www.wildapricot.com)
- o If you are using word processing software without online sharing options, convert the report to PDF and attach it and any support materials to an e-mail. Type a short transmittal message in the e-mail screen.
- *File the report for future reference* after distributing the minutes to meeting participants. Also, file the meeting agenda and other related materials.
  - o In some formal situations, you may be required to print the minutes on acid-free paper and place them in a binder.
  - o As a rule, save files of meeting minutes in a separate folder on your computer, using file and folder names that include meeting dates. Then backup those files on an external drive or in the cloud.

Currently, the proportion of work time spent in meetings is about 35% for middle managers and 50% for upper managers.[55] One study found that the average business employee attends 62 meetings a month, of which half are ineffective. That fact translates to roughly 31 lost hours per person per month—or $37 billion a year in misused salary costs.[56]

One of the most valuable contributions you can make to your organization is to ensure that your meetings are necessary, well planned, and carefully recorded.

Summary

A routine report is a short, simple one that you prepare as part of your normal work role. Most routine reports are prepared often by many individuals covering the same categories of information. Therefore, many organizations use standard forms for them. While some organizations use paper forms, many create standard forms from templates in their database, spreadsheet, or word processing software. Still others create forms using forms automation software, such as Canvas Mobile Forms, Fat Finger, and Snappii Mobile Apps.

To design an effective form, use this checklist.

☐ Form looks simple and uncluttered and includes a heading.
☐ Form includes instructions and a form number.
☐ Form contains adequate space for entering required data.
☐ Column headings (if any) are descriptive and understandable.
☐ Design applies repetition, proximity, contrast, and alignment principles.
☐ Electronic form uses content controls (checkboxes, date pickers, drop-down lists, and text boxes) appropriately.

Besides using forms, business people write routine reports as e-mail messages and memos. Simple reports usually have a direct structure, starting with a general statement followed by details to back it up. To organize report paragraphs, choose from the patterns shown in Figure 1.19.

You may opt for a combination pattern when organizing a routine report, blending two patterns from the list.

Effective reports help your readers understand them as you expected and act as you wanted. The best way to achieve that aim: Ensure that your reports match the needs and goals of the people who read them.

To accomplish this purpose--	Use this organization pattern--
To discuss conditions and predict an outcome	Cause and effect
To organize by time units	Chronological
To examine features of two or more items to show similarities or differences	Comparison or contrast
To describe an obstacle and propose a way around it	Problem-solution
To organize information by units of space or location	Spatial
To organize information without using one of the patterns listed above	Topical

Figure 1.19 Patterns for organizing reports

To write a successful report, make sure it contains the characteristics in this checklist.

- ☐ Accuracy. All numbers and visuals in the report are 100% correct. You have proofed and edited carefully to eliminate any errors in word choice, spelling, punctuation, and grammar.
- ☐ Clarity. Report flows smoothly from beginning to end. The receiver will be able to read and understand effortlessly.
- ☐ Completeness. Report includes all the information the reader will need to understand it and respond suitably.
- ☐ Conciseness. Report includes all the other qualities on this list, using the fewest words necessary to do so.
- ☐ Consideration (empathy). You made every effort to identify with the reader, and your report shows regard for her or his needs and feelings.

A good report format is attractive and functional, inviting readers to read and respond.

You may find the following checklist helpful for formatting e-mail reports.

☐ Include a strong subject line—several descriptive words.

☐ Use headings and spacing to show organization of your e-mail content.

☐ Use one medium or large sans serif font.

☐ Omit paragraph indentations and insert a blank line below each paragraph.

☐ Use bullets appropriately to emphasize key information.

A company may adopt standards for its printed reports and expect all writers in the organization to meet those standards. In the absence of such standards, use this checklist to evaluate format of your memos.

☐ Choose one serif font in size 10 to 14. Size 12 is recommended.

☐ Limit use of ALL CAPS, bold, italics, and underlining. Add emphasis with bullet points, numbered items, and shaded text.

☐ Use single spacing, or some variation of it, for paragraphs.

☐ Omit indentations and leave a blank line below each paragraph.

Each report format involves slightly different specifications and guidelines. You may find the following checklist helpful.

Memo format conventions:

☐ Include guidewords in the memo heading: To, From, Date, and Subject and often Cc (copy).

☐ Omit courtesy and professional titles on the To and From lines unless otherwise indicated.

☐ Use position titles on the From and To lines if you are new to the job.

In modern business, the following types of routine reports are most common:

- Production and performance reports
- Progress and status reports
- Meeting reports
- Trip (travel) reports

Most jobs require production reports periodically to let managers know whether individuals and teams are meeting performance goals. These reports usually include the information on this checklist.

- ☐ Quantitative data, such as units produced or sold, revenue generated, or new customers enlisted
- ☐ Remarks about the work experience, including problems, solutions, and notable successes
- ☐ Work plan for the next period, along with any concerns about it
- ☐ Request for added resources, which may include materials, personnel, supplies, or training

Progress reports include information about a project's schedule and budget, informing readers whether a project will be completed on time and with or without cost overruns. Using bullet points and visuals, a progress report describes the current condition of the project, with an estimated completion date, the costs incurred so far, and an estimate of funding needed to finish.

PPP—which stands for progress, plans, and problems—is a specific and concise, way of reporting daily, weekly, or monthly progress.

Include these three sections.

- Under the Progress heading, list three to five accomplishments since the previous report.
- Under Plans, list three to five goals for the next period.

- Under Problems, list a similar number of specific concerns you have for the project's future, including any assistance or additional resources you think you will need.

To ensure your PPP report is both concise and informative, use this checklist.

- ☐ Apply bold to the heading above each list of bullet points.
- ☐ Write abbreviated sentences (like newspaper headlines) instead of complete ones.
- ☐ Use parallel form in each list. Starting each item with an action verb works well.
- ☐ Include identifying information at the beginning and a summary at the end.

Business people typically spend a large portion of each workday in meetings. Two reports are used routinely to convey meeting information.

- Meeting agenda—announces a meeting and provides a list of events to occur during it
- Meeting minutes—summarizes outcomes of a meeting (discussions, decisions, and tasks assigned)

Meetings may be formal or informal. Formal meetings have a fixed structure and use definite rules, including Robert's Rules of Order. Informal meetings, including most work meetings, are less structured and not driven by rules. For a formal or informal meeting, a good agenda includes all the information meeting participants need to prepare for a productive session.

Use this checklist to plan a meeting agenda.

- ☐ Write out the meeting's purpose and goals.
- ☐ Identify a narrow range of discussion topics that support the purpose and goals.

- [ ] Invite only people whose work involves the meeting topics.
- [ ] Set the meeting date far enough ahead that participants have time to think about the agenda items. If they will need supporting materials, provide them with the agenda.
- [ ] Include your contact information in case of questions about the agenda.
- [ ] Set a day and time when most participants are available. Keep participants in other time zones in mind when scheduling a web conference.
- [ ] Keep each meeting as short as possible—rarely over 90 minutes.
- [ ] Include a time limit for each agenda item (and stick to it).
- [ ] Meet face to face on company premises if all participants work in the same location. Otherwise, you might hold a virtual meeting (web conference) instead of making participants travel to a single location.

Every group that holds meetings should name someone to take notes during the meeting, prepare a report, and distribute those minutes to meeting participants. In general, action minutes are used to summarize work-group (informal) meetings, while discussion minutes are used to summarize professional association (formal) meetings. Action minutes omit discussion and include achievements, decisions, and assignments. Discussion minutes also include achievements and decisions, along with a summary of the discussion leading to them. All meeting minutes include the date, location, and time of the meeting; names of the participants and absentees; and announcement of the next meeting, if known.

If you are the note taker who will subsequently prepare minutes, the following checklist may be helpful.

Did you take the following steps before the meeting?

- [ ] Studied the meeting agenda and previous minutes.
- [ ] Made a glossary of names and abbreviations from the agenda items.

☐ Reviewed Robert's Rules of Order if a formal meeting,
☐ Arrived at the meeting early to set up for reliable note taking.
☐ Checked participants' names on a checklist as they arrived and noted absentees.
☐ Confirmed the presence of a quorum if required.

Remember to do these things during the meeting.

☐ Record decisions, achievements, and action items instantly.
☐ Clarify decisions before the leader moves on to the next agenda item.
☐ Stay neutral in disagreements.
☐ Mentally summarize your notes when not writing them.

As soon as the meeting is adjourned, use this checklist.

☐ Immediately clear up any questions that remain.
☐ Draft the minutes as soon as you can.
☐ Revise the report to ensure clarity and objectivity.
☐ Edit to ensure accuracy and conciseness.
☐ Using a standard format, make the report attractive and the information easy to find.
☐ Enlist someone to edit your revised, edited, and formatted report. In addition, ask the meeting leader to review and approve the minutes.
☐ Distribute your minutes within 24 hours (think of 48 hours as a maximum), using the most efficient medium available.
☐ File the report for future reference, along with the meeting agenda and related materials.

In your concise and factual travel reports, cite the advantages of each trip to your organization. Thus, the reader can decide whether to approve similar trips for you and others in your company. Separately, provide a list of the travel expenses you incurred. Some businesses use standard expense forms or spreadsheets. Increasingly, business travelers compile a travel expense profile, using expense reporting software, such as Abacus, Concur, and ExpensAble.

Production, progress, meeting, and trip reports are routine in the sense that they are prepared regularly. Even so, they are important to your organization's success—and the success of your career.

CHAPTER 2

Writing Nonroutine Reports

The need to write or read reports differs for everyone almost daily. As you carry out your work, you sometimes confront circumstances, make decisions, or take actions that deviate from your normal routine yet fall within your range of responsibility. These situations often require that you report your actions or decisions to upper-level management, your subordinates, or even to the public or stockholders. Those reports may be classified as *nonroutine* reports.

Naturally, this book cannot illustrate all nonroutine reports that you may encounter. However, it will present the following nonroutine reports that you might send and receive.

- Interview reports: individual job applicant, focus group
- Recommendation reports: justification report, feasibility report
- Public relations (PR) reports: press release, fact sheet, and backgrounder
- Marketing reports: whitepaper and business proposal
- Summaries: abstract, overview, and executive summary

Interview Reports

Although you may not interview people regularly in your job, you may occasionally be requested to interview a job applicant to your company. Additionally, you may now and then be on a special project team that requires you to obtain critical information by interviewing a group of people. In both cases, rather than provide verbatim transcripts of your interviews, you will likely be expected to condense the information you obtained in a report to whomever asked you to conduct the interview.

Individual's Interview Report

Appropriate content for an interview report includes the following information.

- When, where, and how the interview was conducted
- Summary of the information obtained
- Relevant comments about the interview experience, such as problems encountered or recommendations related to interview procedure.

Figure 2.1 demonstrates an interview report for an individual job applicant.

Figure 2.1 Interview report for individual job applicant

Interview Summary. Mr. Burnitz arrived on time and properly attired for interview. He greeted me with a handshake and smile. The applicant demonstrated good posture when seated and leaned in and made frequent eye contact as we conversed about the job and his fitness for it.
Mr. Burnitz said he performed satisfactorily at production tasks in Cavort's Production Room A for the past 15 months (October, 2017), and text from his supervisor immediately after the interview rated his work "above satisfactory." He also had relevant production experience at Champion for four months prior to coming here.
Applicant's knowledge of Cavort Sportwear in relation to competitors is weak, as is his knowledge of the sports and sportwear industries in relation to the U.S. economy. Mr. Burnitz acknowledged that he did not view these subjects as priorities while learning the ropes in production; but as a supervisor, he would welcome deeper knowledge in these areas.
When asked how he would handle unproductive employees who would/could not carry their weight, the applicant responded thoughtfully, noting that he'd start by analyzing whether additional training, equipment, or other resources might rectify the problem. His answer was thorough and showed considerable human relations skills.
Mr. Burnitz also asked me several appropriate questions, including about career pathways leading to management positions in this organization. I see this as a sign of his ambition and motivation that would serve Cavort in the near future and perhaps later on, too.
I believe Mr. Burnitz is a worthy candidate for Production Supervisor, Room C; and I would like to see him awarded the position. *Stacy Costello*

Figure 2.1 (Continued)

Following these guidelines will help you write an effective interview report.[1]

- *Introduction.* State the subject's name and position applied for, along with the date, time, and location of the interview. In addition, state how you expect the interview information to be used and why you conducted the interview, since interviewing job applicants is not one of your regular duties.
- *Discussion.* Give a summary of topics discussed in the interview. Also, comment on the nature, or themes, of the applicant's answers, without going into detail.

- *Findings.* Write about your findings during the interview; that is, state what you learned about the job applicant. If the interview revealed unexpected information that is altogether relevant to the interview's purpose, discuss that information briefly.
- *Circumstances.* Write about the interview context, too. Explain any ways that the setting—such as distracting noises or blasts of cold air—may have affected the interview. Comment on the interviewee's behavior, mannerisms, and reactions to your questions.
- *Summary.* Recap the report, emphasizing your major findings. Restate your plans for using the information gathered in the interview.

Focus Group's Interview Report

Focus group interviews are often used to determine interest in a new product or service, the effectiveness of advertising and communications research, background studies on consumers' frames of reference, or consumer attitudes and behaviors toward an idea, organization, and so on.[2]

The standard focus group interview involves six to twelve similar individuals—such as male customers, young professionals, or those who regularly purchase a certain laundry detergent—who are brought together to discuss a topic. The respondents are selected according to the relevant sampling plan and meet at a central location that has equipment to make an audio or audiovisual record of the discussion. *Note*: In recent years, online focus groups have been increasingly useful for consumer research. An interviewer, also called a facilitator or moderator, invites vetted interviewees to sign into a web conference at a pre-arranged time and to participate in an online focus group.[3]

In face-to-face and online focus groups, the facilitator keeps discussion moving and focused on the topic. Usually the interviewer also analyzes the transcript or recording of the session and prepares a summary of the meeting. Figure 2.2 shows a focus group interview report.

Both interview reports provide the information necessary for others to evaluate the interviews and to act on them.

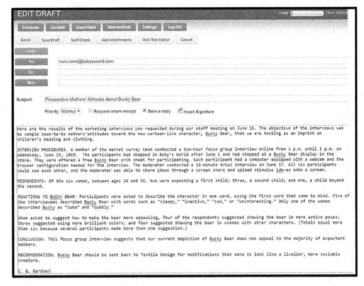

Figure 2.2 Focus group interview report

Recommendation-Based Reports

A feasibility report analyzes the potential success of a major undertaking. A justification report describes or proposes an action and gives reasons for that action. In both reports, the person reporting recommends action and provides supporting data.

Feasibility Reports

Feasibility report is the term often used to identify a special type of recommendation report, which analyzes the potential success of a major undertaking. Feasibility studies are often conducted before a company commits itself to a large capital investment, a new product or service, or a new plant location. A feasibility study involves three questions.

1. Is the undertaking technically possible?
2. Is the undertaking achievable within budget?
3. Will the undertaking do what it is supposed to do and also be profitable?

Although most feasibility studies result in lengthy, analytical reports, some feasibility reports are presented as short reports. For example, analyzing the feasibility of opening a textile manufacturing plant in Honduras would surely require considerable research and analysis and would result in a lengthy report. In contrast, analyzing the feasibility of changing the hours of operation of a local restaurant would require considerably less data collection and analysis, and the result could be presented in a short-report format.

A feasibility report must contain the following information.[4]

- *Description of the project under consideration.* A description includes these topics.
  - o Scope of the project
  - o What the project will accomplish and how it will do so
  - o How stakeholders will be affected
  - o A timeline for completion and a breakdown of tasks (what, when, by whom)
- *An unequivocal recommendation to proceed with the project or recede from it.*
- *Data to support the recommendation.*

The person requesting the report is primarily interested in the recommendation—whether positive or negative. Therefore, feasibility reports usually present the recommendation at or near the beginning of the report. Figure 2.3 shows an unusually short feasibility report. *Note*: The report is shown in business letter format. Information about letter format follows Figure 2.3. Meanwhile, notice the feasibility report's, content, and writing style.

As noted, Figure 2.3 demonstrates letter format, used for external reports of one to three pages. (If a report exceeds three pages, it should be produced in manuscript format, as shown in Appendix B.)

This specific format is called block because all parts of the letter are aligned on the left. As you review the report again, notice the parts and their sequence, which apply to all business letters. Figure 2.4 describes each letter part.

Justification Reports

Generally, routine reports (Chapter 1), interview reports, and feasibility reports are requested by the reader. However, justification reports are almost always initiated by the writer. For example, an automobile manufacturer notifies auto owners that they should take their cars to a dealership to check for a possible defect in the steering mechanism. This notice is a justification report: The manufacturer requests a

---

MARKET SCOPE, INC.
P.O. Box 1584
MADISON, WI 53713-1584

April 24, 2019

Ms. Heather Bhatt
107 Marlene Dr.
Marshall, MN 56258

Feasibility of Mail-Order Business: Women's Fashions

In January, you asked that I conduct a study of the feasibility of your beginning a "mail-order boutique" to market fashionable, easy-care clothing to career women in the 35–50 age range. You planned to operate that business from Marshall, MN, with an initial investment of not more than $1.5 million.

Recommendation

I recommend that you **not** launch the mail-order business you proposed. Current projections suggest that you will suffer a substantial loss during three years of operation even with relatively optimistic projections. Furthermore, competition from catalog sales grows continuously along with burgeoning web sales, with the number of small companies up almost 60% in the past five years. Establishing a website to complement the catalog is an imperative. Therefore, the very real risk exists that at the end of three years you will be looking at the loss of your $1.5 million investment in addition to an operating loss of more than $480,000.

You can currently invest your money in moderate-risk Exchange Traded Funds (ETFs), some of which have earned 8% to 9% annually in recent years. Assuming an average annual return of 8.5% on such an investment, at the end of three years, your money will have grown by more than $400,000.

Findings

Here are the findings that justify my recommendation.

Projected first-year costs and revenues

The first year of operation will require that you conduct marketing tests to establish your customer base; locate and buy appropriate merchandise; develop, print, and mail catalogs; build a website; pay salaries; and cover bad debts and returns. If you send out 500,000 catalogs, you can anticipate that 1% of the recipients will respond with an average order of $112, generating $560,000 in sales.

Figure 2.3 Feasibility report

Ms. Heather Bhatt   - 2-   April 24, 2019

Your costs to generate those sales are projected as follows:

Catalog development/market tests	$ 67,000
Printing and mailing	310,000
Website development	8,000
Salaries (marketing, merchandising, customer service, telemarketing)	280,000
Cost of merchandise (45–55% of sales)	280,000
Bad debts/returns (1% of sales)	6,000
Total	$ 951,000

As you can see, your loss from operations would be over $390,000 during the first year.

Projected second-year costs and revenues

If you do not increase your catalog distribution but rely on web sales for growth, catalog development costs will decline slightly; but your printing and mailing costs will likely increase. Personnel costs will increase also; but we are assuming that with efficiencies derived from experience, they will not increase in proportion to sales. Even if sales double in the second year, you will still not generate a profit. To earn $1,120,000 in revenue you will incur the following expenses

Catalog development	$ 57,000
Printing and mailing	336,000
Website maintenance	2,500
Salaries	308,000
Cost of merchandise	560,000
Bad debts/returns	12,000
Total	$1,275,500

Projected third-year costs and revenue

Again, relying on the web for increased sales, you should maintain your catalog development costs in the third year of operation. Again, printing and mailing costs, along with salaries, will likely increase, although not in direct proportion to the increase in sales. As the customer base develops, you may expect increased sales, but likely not as large a percentage as in the second year of operation. Another 50% increase in sales will be necessary to generate a modest profit in the third year. That will bring in revenue of $1,680,000. Related cost projections follow:

Figure 2.3 (Continued)

Ms. Heather Bhatt   - 3 -   April 24, 2019

Catalog development	$ 57,000
Printing and mailing	364,000
Website maintenance	2,500
Salaries	336,000
Cost of merchandise	840,000
Bad debts/returns	18,000
Total	$1,617,500

Summary

To summarize, here is what you can expect during the first three years if you are marginally successful.

Year	Revenue	Expenses	Net
1	$ 560,000	$ 951,000	$ (391,000)
2	1,120,000	1,275,500	(155,500)
3	1,680,000	1,617,500	62,500
Total	$ 3,360,000	$3,840,000	$ (484,000)

Those projections result in a net loss of over $480,000 during the first three years of operation. In contrast, if you were to invest your $1.5 million in an EFT averaging 8.5% per annum, you would see a gain of approximately $405,000.

Additional Comments

I have enjoyed doing this study for you. If you are interested in an analysis of another entrepreneurial opportunity, please call me.

Sincerely

Heidi Fitzpatrick

Heidi Fitzpatrick
Entrepreneurial Consultant

Figure 2.3   (Concluded)

Business Letter Component	Description
Sender's identification	In the absence of a company letterhead, type your organization's complete mailing address an inch or so down the page. Use a letterhead for the first page only; after that, use plain paper with this heading: receiver's name, page number, and date.
Date written or mailed	Put the date a few blank lines below a letterhead or immediately below a return address. Spell out the month; type the day as a cardinal number (10, not 10th), and the four-digit year: February 15, 2019. International formats for dates may vary.
Receiver's address	Place the complete letter address several lines below the date. Use a courtesy or professional title with the person's name; but omit these titles if you do not know the person's gender or a woman's title preference.
	Include the receiver's position title; put it beside the name (comma between) or on the next line.
	Remove excess space between lines of the address.
Salutation	Start the greeting with Dear. If the letter address contains a courtesy or professional title, use it with the person's last name only.
	Use a first-name-only greeting only if you know the person well. Consider omitting the salutation and the complimentary close, when the address lacks a person's name.
Letter body (message)	Do not indent paragraphs; do insert blank space between them. After the first page, begin each page with a heading, including the first line of the receiver's address, the page number, and the date as shown on page 1. This heading may appear on one line or in a three-line block:
	Ms. J. B. McCarthy Page 2 February 15, 2019

Figure 2.4 Business letter parts and sequence

specific action and provides reasons for it. These reports differ from the others we have discussed in another way: Justification reports involve persuading readers in addition to informing them.

Complimentary close	Leave a blank line below the letter body, or message.
	Use a traditional close: Sincerely is a good choice as it fits in both formal and informal situations.
Your signature lines	Leave a couple blank lines below the complimentary close, above your name.
	Type your name and position title or department affiliation beside your name (comma between) or immediately under it.
	Sign the letter in the space above your typed name.
Prepare for sending	To send via <u>USPS</u>, fold and insert the letter into a window envelope OR print the letter address near the horizontal and vertical center of a standard envelope. If using a plain envelope (nothing preprinted on it), print your name, company name, and business address in the upper-left corner.
	To mail letters using an <u>online application</u>, choose from these sites.
	• FlyDoc (https://www.esker.com/ business-process-solutions/automation-products/flydoc-online-fax-service)
	• Docaway (https://www.docsaway.com/goto/mail_documents.php)
	• LetterStream (https://www.letterstream .com/letter-options)
	• Mail A Letter (www.mailaletter.com)
	To send via <u>email</u>, convert the word processing file to a PDF (preserves letter format through all networks); then attach it to an email, complete with subject line and a one-line message calling attention to the attachment.

Figure 2.4 (Continued)

Use the following nine-step strategy to write persuasively.[5]

1. *Picture the reader of your report sitting across a table from you.* Will that person be amenable to the content of your report, or will he or she be opposed to it? If opposed, what objections do you anticipate? Also think about that person's greatest interests and concerns—both the logical thoughts (like competitiveness, productivity, profitability, return on investment, and risk management) and the emotions, or values (like social approval, sense of

belonging, happiness, personal security, and self-fulfillment). As you begin drafting your report, write to this one person only. You will consider secondary readers when revising your draft.

2. *Most of the time use direct structure, starting your draft with a clear, simple, and strong statement of your recommendation or request.* Some writers suggest starting with a disarming question that you can answer later in the report or an attention-grabbing quotation that you can expand on. If you have any doubts about the aptness of such an opening in our case or your ability to handle it expertly, start with a declarative sentence. *Note*: If you sense your recommendation or request may astound or baffle your reader, use indirect structure. In that instance, establish your credibility first and identify a problem needing a solution before stating your recommendation or request.

3. *Give compelling arguments, or reasons—from the reader's viewpoint—why your recommendation or request is important.* Assume the person reading your report wants an answer to this question: What's in it for me and this organization? To build your case, appeal to the reader's logical interests and her or his emotional concerns. Make one primary and the other secondary, according to which dominates the reader's view.

4. *Next, provide detailed support for your arguments to enhance your credibility* and help the reader see the matter from your viewpoint. The amount of support needed depends on whether the reader will be amenable or resistant to your recommendation or request. But to persuade, the support must be vivid. Use word pictures and visuals appropriately.

    Cite research results; quote opinions from recognizable experts and reputable publications. Cite examples from your own related experiences and observations.

5. *Now, evaluate the merits of your position and any evidence against it.* Include findings that contradict the support you provided and quote authorities who disagree with you. Doing so may seem self-defeating, but your willingness to consider opposing viewpoints enhances your credibility and strengthens your position.

If you have not already done so, offset each reader objection that you anticipated.

6. *Discuss the financials.* As thoroughly as you can, identify the resources that will be needed to implement your recommendation or request. Also, estimate the cost savings of your recommendation or the revenue you expect it to generate.

7. *Recap your recommendation or request and indicate the response you want from the reader.* Make it very clear and as easy as you can for her or him to comply with your recommendation or request.

8. *Return to the beginning and draft an appropriate subject line* for your report. If your report uses direct structure, hint at your recommendation or request in the subject line. However, if your report uses indirect structure, describe the report in broader terms, omitting even a hint of your recommendation or request.

9. *After a day or two, rigorously revise your report draft.* Be especially careful with the following aspects of your draft.

- Have you written from the primary reader's point of view? Consider the secondary readers: Do you need to supply additional information for them? Might they have objections that are different from the primary reader's objections? Do you need to increase the number of emotional or logical appeals?
- Is every piece of support very detailed and pertinent to your recommendation or request? Have facts been verified at the source? For example, each study cited does exist and its outcomes are exactly what you stated.
- Did you confirm all your numerical data and calculations?
- In your arguments, have you avoided the common fallacies (errors in logic) listed in Figure 2.5.
- Does your report have a personal and positive tone? And did you write concisely (fewest words)? Are the other report characteristics discussed in Chapter 1 present in your report?

Fallacy Type	Also Called	Description
Diversion	Red herring	Distracted the reader by presenting an unrelated argument
False analogy	Apples and oranges	Drew a comparison between two dissimilar subjects
False cause	Post Hoc, Ergo Propter Hoc	Claimed that Event A caused Event B because Event A occurred first
False dilemma	Either-Or fallacy	Discussed a problem as if only two possible solutions exist
Hasty generalization	---	Drew conclusions from a too-small or unrepresentative sample
Personal attack	Ad hominem attack	Attacked a person rather than her or his reasoning

Figure 2.5 Common logical fallacies

A justification report appears in Figure 2.6. Notice how the nine-step persuasive strategy has been applied here.

Public Relations (Publicity) Reports

In the business world, PR is communication designed to create and maintain goodwill between an organization and its publics (current and prospective customers, employees, partners, stockholders, suppliers, and others). PR takes a variety of forms, but the most recognizable form is publicity: newsworthy company information distributed by traditional mass media (newspapers, magazines, radio, and TV), blogs, podcasts, and social media to gain favorable public attention. Publicity, unlike advertising and direct marketing, spreads information about a company for free.[6]

Large organizations typically have a corporate communication division that is responsible for PR, or the company hires a PR professional at a PR agency or marketing firm. A key function of a PR professional is creating media kits (also called press kits) for clients. A media kit contains various reports, each with a unique purpose, assembled to provide

---

BAE SYSTEMS
INSPIRED WORK

To: Ian Imani

From: Kimberly Keaton   *kk*

Date: July 26, 2019

Subject: Approval to Attend 2019 APM Conference

This year's Alliance of Project Managers (APM) is set for October 13-15 in Las Vegas, and I want to be one of the 500 project managers in attendance.

Conference sessions will focus on ways to integrate business management techniques into project management, which I would find extremely valuable and could immediately apply to my work. Conference attendees will represent many fields, including energy, financial services, healthcare, manufacturing, professional services, technology/software, and telecommunications, and, of course, other defense and aerospace companies. The conference will give me a chance to meet and share ideas with many of them.

Several of the sessions will offer strategies that I can implement as soon as I return to the office on October 16. A few of the sessions that interest me most include presentations on the **Agile method** of project management **versus** the more traditional **Waterfall method**. These sessions would give me insight into each method and enable me to choose the better method for each project I manage in the future.

Sessions are presented by recognized experts in the project management community, for example:

- "Apply PPP to the Projects You Manage" by Dr. Martha Thomas
- "Best Practices for the Evolving PMO" by John Santa Barbara.

By attending these sessions, I can make lasting connections with these thought-leaders that will be beneficial to me and BAE now and later. In addition, by attending this three-day conference, I will receive 24 professional development units (PDUs) toward maintaining my certification with Project Management Institute (PMI).

The exhibit area will feature over a hundred exhibitors of products designed to facilitate project management. I will have an opportunity to meet with many of these company representatives and discuss their products and services, eliminating the time and expense of future trips to each vendor separately.

This conference offers the best value with a registration fee of $1,199 for one participant. If I enroll by August 18, I can save $200 with the Early Bird discount. Also, **if multiple people from the company register** at the same time, we can receive even **deeper discounts** ($900 per person). My request is for conference registration, travel costs, and food and lodging. APM has arranged for room discounts at several hotels surrounding the convention center, and lunch and breakfast are provided each day for which I register. Also, an evening networking event the first day will include heavy hors d'oeuvres, which will be adequate for my dinner.

Attending the APM conference this October would be a valuable experience for me; more importantly, it would greatly benefit this organization. I will be able to bring home all conference materials to share with others in the office and possibly train coworkers if needed. Of course, I will also send you a trip report.

Figure 2.6 Justification report

information about an organization to reporters. We will discuss three components: press release, fact sheet, and backgrounder. Though press kits vary widely, the main report in every kit is the press, or media, release. *Note*: For information about other kit components, see blogs by Duncan,[7] Ferreira,[8] and Tapia.[9]

Press Release

A press release—also called media release, news release, and press state-ment—is a report announcing notable information to the news media and beyond. Small businesses and nonprofit organizations usually forego a media kit. Instead, press releases are prepared by managers and submit-ted directly for publication.

Occasions calling for a press release include the following examples.[10]

- Introducing a new partnership
- Launching a new product
- Opening a new office
- Promoting or hiring a new executive
- Rebranding (creating a new identity for an established brand by changing its name, logo, or packaging, or a combination of these features)
- Receiving an award
- Updating existing products

An effective press release contains the following information:

- Name of organization releasing the news
- Target date for publication of the news
- A headline that states the core of the story
- The information source, when applicable
- Answers to the basic communication questions: Who? What? When? Where? Why? How?
- Name of person to contact for further information, along with phone or fax number and e-mail address

The body of the press release should be organized in an inverted pyramid form: Answers to basic questions appear first, followed by supporting details. This structure permits the reporter to cut the story without deleting vital facts. Figure 2.7 shows an effective structure and format for a press release. (The two-page release probably would be sent as an e-mail attachment.)

FOR RELEASE
April 19, 2019

CONTACT: Emily Watts 843.805.3053

PR & Publications Director
Charleston Metro Chamber of Commerce

Boeing Gives $140,000 Grant to The Education Foundation for STEAM Education

April 16, 2019 - Charleston, SC – The Education Foundation received $139,000 grant from The Boeing Company today to develop and implement a plan for aligning Science, Technology, Engineering, Arts, and Mathematics (STEAM) education in Berkeley, Charleston and Dorchester Counties with workforce needs. The goal of the "STEAM in the Workplace" initiative is to ensure a pipeline of graduates who are equipped with knowledge and skills that match our region's economic needs.

The Boeing funds will allow The Education Foundation to provide professional development for teachers of STEAM disciplines in three ways: teachers will gain on-site experience in STEAM-related businesses; participate in teaching institutes that focus on project-based learning; and implement new methods for teaching STEAM to their students.

The growing need for STEAM education is largely due to the rapid growth of STEAM-related industries globally in recent years. Because STEAM industries like Boeing are expanding worldwide, it is crucial to educate students in these fields to provide companies with a competitive workforce.

By doing "externships" in the region's businesses, teachers will see STEAM in action, learn first-hand about workplace requirements and simultaneously gain a wealth of ideas for student projects. The practical business experience will be followed by training in project-based learning. The core idea behind project-based learning is that real-world problems capture students' interest and stimulate critical thinking and teamwork as the students apply new knowledge in a problem-solving context. The "STEAM in the Workplace" initiative will give the 60 participating teachers a new arsenal of project-based teaching strategies aimed at preparing students for entry-level jobs that are becoming more and more sophisticated.

- more –

Figure 2.7 Press release

"Most teachers go directly from their own education into teaching. This program gives teachers a chance to see and work within the business world and then translate those experiences into 'real world' learning experiences for students." says David Ramey, chairman of The Education Foundation.

There are multiple exit points for students in STEAM-related fields, so whether students want to continue their studies through higher education at a 4-year or 2-year college or enter the workforce directly after graduating high school, opportunities are available for them to pursue their goals and interests in STEAM. In addition, STEAM education increases employability for students and reduces training time and cost for employers. "STEAM in the Workplace" will address a critical regional need by preparing students for success in a work world that increasingly demands high-level skills in science, technology, engineering, the arts, and math.

"STEAM in the Workplace" is guided by a steering committee made up of business and education leaders. The committee is currently engaging the support of STEAM-related businesses who will offer two-day externships to teachers in the summer of 2019. Businesses interested in participating should contact Angie Rylands, The Education Foundation's Regional STEAM Coordinator, at arylands@edfound.net.

About The Education Foundation: The Education Foundation, an initiative of the Charleston Metro Chamber of Commerce was founded in 1995 to build partnerships between the metro business community and the public schools, mobilize resources and advocate the changes necessary in our community to prepare all students for careers of the future. Additional information and photos available at our website (www. theeducationfoundation.org).

###

Figure 2.7 (Continued)

Observe these standard components of a printed press release and the placement of each part.[11]

- *The release date appears at the upper-left,* about 1.5 in. from the top edge starting at the left margin. Customarily, this information is typed in ALL CAPS.
  - o Businesses often send an embargoed press release, meaning the report is shared with the media in advance of its publishing date. For example, the report in Figure 2.7 was sent on April 16 with this information: FOR RELEASE ON APRIL 19.
  - o In the case of broadcast and online media, the desired hour of release also may be specified.
- *Contact information is prominently displayed* as shown in Figure 2.7. (Some journalists, however, prefer the contact information at the end of the report.) The name of a contact person and her or his e-mail address may suffice. Provide additional means of contact unless you know from experience that the reporters you release to rely on e-mail.
- *Next the headline is centered in bold.* The first word and all proper nouns are capitalized; most headline words are lowercase. A subheading in italics may be placed below the headline, with a blank line between headings. *Note*: If sending your release by e-mail, begin the headline at the left edge of your screen (not centered).
- *Double spacing is conventional* throughout the body of a printed release, providing space for a reporter to jot notes. In double-spaced text, the first line of each paragraph is indented a half inch. *Note*: If sending your release by e-mail, do not double space. Instead follow the guides in Chapter 1 for e-mail format.
- *The current date and city in which the press release originates* appears just before the announcement. Naming the city of origin locates your company's brand, helping to establish its identity.

- *The word END is centered below the report body.* Alternatively, the ending can be indicated by these centered characters: ### (three number signs or hash tags).

Guides to Writing a Press Release

This list of best practices will help you write effective press releases. Whether you send a printed or e-mail release, post it on your company's website media page, or post it to a media distribution service, these guides will help you achieve good results time after time.[12]

- *Confine your press release to 300 to 500 words*—one or possibly two double-spaced pages.
- *When sending a printed press release, use your company letterhead* (8.5-in. by 11-in. paper with a printed heading showing the organization's name, and contact information, such as USPS address, phone and FAX numbers, and web address.) When e-mailing a release, prepare it in e-mail format, not as an attachment.
- *Grab a blogger's or journalist's attention with your headline.* (Reporters usually change the headline to appeal to their audience.) Include your organization's name in the headline and a hook to incite a desire for more information.
  - But write the report first; THEN write the headline, using keywords from the release.
  - Use no more than 100 characters in the headline, including well-known abbreviations and acronyms.
  - Type the headline in a large, bold font.
- *Cover the 5Ws and the H (who, what, when, where, why, and how) in the first paragraph. Note*: In an online setting, to have your press release indexed by Google, fit all vital information into the first 65 words (the maximum word count that shows in Google search results).
- *Next, include an enticing quotation from one or two key executives* that emphasize the main point of your report.

- o Always include a job title for each person quoted.
- o The material in quotation marks does not need to be an actual quote, but it should seem authentic.
- o Be sure each person quoted is satisfied with the comment attributed to her or him.
- *Then, give details that strengthen your report,* such as future implications of your announcement or its impact on the local economy.
- *Include a call to action*—what you would like the blogger or journalist to do—and make it easy for her or him to comply. In Figure 2.7, the last sentence is a call to action.
- *Write concisely, using relatively short paragraphs and bulleted lists.*
  - o Omit buzzwords (important-sounding, but mostly meaningless, words or phrase used mainly to impress), hype (exaggerated or fake publicity), and jargon (special vocabulary used by a specific group, such as business jargon or medical jargon).[13] If you cannot avoid using a technical term, define it.
  - o Maintain a positive tone, avoiding references to negative events, such as "a slump in demand following Hurricane Harvey" or "sudden departure of the former CEO."
- *Consider using an online press release builder for text-only releases.* The following list identifies several examples.
  - o Automatic Press Release Builder (http://videomarketerstheme.com/wp-content/themes/WP-Social-Press/form)
  - o Bill Myers Online (https://bmyers.com/public/541.cfm)
  - o Instant Press Release (https://ducttapemarketing.com/instant-press-release)
  - o Xtensio (https://xtensio.com/press-release)
- *If you cite statistical data, cite or link to your references.*
- *Use relevant visuals* (graphs, infographics, photos, or tables, for example) and refer to each visual in your text. Visuals serve the following purposes.[14]

- o Emphasize major points and separate them from minor points
  - o Clarify information that words alone can hardly express
  - o Reinforce the report narrative
  - o Aid reader retention and recall of information
  - o Summarize essential information while omitting nonessential details
  - o Attract attention and add interest
  - o Improve believability by lending a sense of exactness
- If including a graph or table, send your original spreadsheet or word processing file. If sending a photo, make it a high-resolution image, saved to a flash drive. (Some news services charge extra for publishing visual content.) *Note*: Of course, a social media news release (SMNR) (discussion begins on page 92) involves multimedia, including animations, audio, interactive content, and video.
- To facilitate the production of effective visuals, become familiar with one or more of these online graphic design apps.
  - o Canva (https://.canva.com)
  - o DesignBold (https://.designbold.com)
  - o Fotor (https://.fotor.com)
  - o PiktoChart (https://piktochart.com)
  - o Snappa (https://snappa.com)
  - o Stencil (https://getstencil.com).
- Following your announcement (report), give information about your company and its policies that you pick up from the organization's business plan, brochures, newsletters, presentation slide decks, and so on. *Note*: This information is called boilerplate (any text that can be reused in new settings or for new purposes without being changed much from the original).[15]
- *Publish your press release on your organization's website or your blog or both.* Then provide the complete URL (not an embedded link) of the website at or near the end of your printed or e-mail release.

- o Ideally, your company's website includes a media page accessible only to journalists. The page should contain media kit components and a database of all publicity released to date.
- o Share each media release with your followers on social media, too.
- o Additionally, if the media pick up your news, share their news reports with your social media followers.
- *Make sure your release is well written and error-free.* *Note*: If a blogger or journalist recognizes a content error as such, he or she probably will discard the release. Otherwise, erroneous information may be on display for all the writer's constituents to see.
  - o For revising your report, ask an associate who does not know the context of your press release to read it and tell you (1) why the report is important, (2) what your organization does, and (3) why the executives quoted were chosen. If your associate cannot answer these questions accurately, revise your press release and repeat the process with another associate.
  - o For editing your report, refer to Appendix A, page 203.
- *For additional insight into writing press releases, view some of the 40 examples* cited in a small-business blog by Orencia.[16]
- *Target a specific audience (market)* by sending your media release to a few select bloggers and journalists.
  - o Identify which journalists your target audience follows.
  - o Also, identify reporters who have experience covering your industry, if not your company. With your release, send a personal message showing how your report connects to the kinds of content they write.
  - o To find the right journalist to pitch your news, use one or more of these PR software sites.
    - Muck Rack (https://muckrack.com)
    - MyPRGenie (http://try.myprgenie.com/prnetwork)
    - Supernewsroom (https://supernewsroom.com)
    - Traacker (www.traackr.com)

- o Once you identify the reporter(s) you will target, determine if he or she follows *The Associated Press Stylebook*,[17] or AP Style, as many journalists do. If so, become familiar with AP standards for press release format, citing references, and writing style. Besides a print version that is updated annually, AP Stylebook is accessible on the web (https://apstylebook.com).

- *Give the reporter a bit of lead time by sending your release under embargo* a day or two before the release date you specify. If transmitting it the same day, put it out early.

- *Consider sending your printed release by FAX or even USPS to distinguish it* from the many e-mailed releases bloggers and journalists receive. *Note*: If you e-mail your report, use the release headline as the e-mail subject line.

- *For wide-ranging circulation of weighty news, consider using a media release distribution service.* A release distribution service can disseminate a single press release to blogger networks, broadcast media, journalists, mobile channels, print media, search engines, social media platforms, and websites. The following list identifies popular press release distribution services. Prices of these services vary. Naturally, the amount you pay should correspond with the importance of your news.

  - o 1888 PressRelease.com (https://1888pressrelease.com)
  - o Business Wire (www.businesswire.com)
  - o Cision PR Newswire (https://prnewswire.com)
  - o eReleases (http://ereleases.com)
  - o Marketwired (marketwired.com)
  - o PR.com (https://pr.com)

The technology company Telit maintains an impressive bank of news releases in its Telit News Center (https://telit.com/about/press-media). Perusing several of them will reveal consistency in organization, writing style, and word choice.

Video News Release (VNR)

A video news release, or VNR, is a press release (usually a 90-second video with voiceover) sent free of charge by satellite link to TV and online newsrooms. VNRs are usually produced by PR professionals and used to cover product innovations, company milestones, and current consumer issues.[18]

Networks and local television stations are free to air the videos or not. Some stations air VNRs as they are presented; most stations use parts of the presentation or take its ideas and build their own stories. To increase the probability of having videos aired, companies should produce them in an objective, newsworthy fashion. To attract the interest of the news media, the story must capture the interest of the average consumer in the viewing audience.

In addition, the following list provides basic VNR production guidelines.

- *Use VNR for major announcements that can be conveyed visually.* High production costs make VNR impractical for minor stories or announcements that lack action and visual appeal.
- *Use images extensively.* Long voiceovers and "talking heads" are uninteresting.
- *Keep the narrator off camera.* Most TV stations avoid showing unfamiliar faces in their news segments.
- *Incorporate interviews and an ample amount of cover footage* (brief film clips that the TV news producers can use to modify your VNR).
- *Make the VNR resemble a real news story*, not an advertisement. Using news announcers, camera crews, producers, and writers makes this more likely.

Television stations are required by the Federal Communication Commission to identify the company or government agency that produces any aired VNR. Ideally, such identification is built into the VNR during production. In addition, the PR professional who produces a VNR should monitor the airing of it to ensure the source is disclosed on air.

Social Media News Release (SMNR)[19]

Much of the foregoing information about press releases applies to
SMNRs. In fact, content of an SMNR can be prepared in the narrative
style depicted in Figure 2.7—with the likely addition of more photos and
links to multimedia. Another way to do an SMNR is to deconstruct it
and send the separate elements—boilerplate, contact information, core
facts, quotations, and audio-visual components (graphics, photos, podcasts, sound bites, and video). Thus, users can combine the elements in
various ways.

Traditionally, press releases have been written with journalists—the
writers of print media—in mind. An SMNR needs to appeal simultaneously to those journalists as well as to bloggers, publishers, and the public.
The main way to add appeal? Limit text; add visual content (infographics,
photos, slides, and videos).

If you decide to create visual content yourself, the following guides
provide aid.

- *Use infographics to convey quantities of data in a way that is
  easy to comprehend and memorable.*
  - o Become thoroughly familiar with your data and the
    story it tells.
  - o Identify what you want readers to take away from your
    infographic.
  - o Sketch a storyboard, laying out the data-story left to
    right and top to bottom.
  - o Choose an online infographics maker such as one of the
    following.
    - Venngage (https://venngage.com)
    - Piktochart (https://piktochart.com)
    - Easel.ly (https://easel.ly)
  - o For the small amount of text involved, use unusual fonts
    that are also very readable.
  - o Choose calm, harmonious colors, avoiding a white back-
    ground and dark and neon colors. The rule of three is

reliable for color selection: three complementary colors with the lightest in the background. If you need more colors, use shades of the original three.

o As a test, ask someone unfamiliar with your data to interpret your infographic.

o As an alternative to creating your own infographics with the help of an online infographics maker, choose a firm that specializes in infographics design. Examples follow.

- Avalaunch (https://avalaunchmedia.com/services/infographics)
- Info Graphic World (http://infographicworld.com)
- Upwork (www.upwork.com)

- *Use photos to capture attention and add interest to your story.*

o Use only extremely relevant, high-resolution photos (achievable using your phone). *Note*: During each day at work, snap and store photos of people on the job. Then the next time you write a news release, you may be able to use photo(s) from that album on your phone.

o Avoid generic stock photos in favor of specific, incomparable ones.

o Include an image preview that downloads quickly.

- *Use presentation slides, a familiar story-telling medium, by posting on a dedicated website, such as SlideShare (https://www.slideshare.net).* Then link to it from your news release.

o Give your slide deck a winning title and a fascinating cover, or title slide.

o Embed links in slides that enable viewers to respond to them.

o While SlideShare has more traffic than any comparable website, many other slide sharing options are available, including the ones listed here.

- authorSTREAM (www.authorstream.com)
- PowerShow (www.powershow.com)
- Scribd (https://www.scribd.com)
- Speaker Deck (https://speakerdeck.com)

- *Use video to draw viewers into your news and identify closely with it; also, to replace copious text for hard-to-explain concepts.*
  - Keep these videos short (a minute or two) and simple. *Note*: Just like for photos, capture videos of activity in the workplace during each workday.
  - Instead of hosting videos on your server, upload your files to Vimeo (https://vimeo.com), YouTube (https://www.youtube.com), or an alternative video hosting site. Doing so will help your video load quicker. Also, search engines will be able to find your video content and list it in users' SRPs (search results pages).
  - Take advantage of a video hosting service to help you with concept development and video production and marketing. A few outstanding examples are listed.
    - Wistia (https://wistia.com)
    - vzaar (https://vzaar.com)
    - videopath (http://videopath.com)
    - Niche (https://nichevid.com)
    - Cincopa (https://cincopa.com)

To see several examples of an SMNR, visit this Prezly web page (https://.prezly.com/press-release-examples).

If you decide not to create SMNRs yourself, do what many business managers do: Turn over SMNR production to your organization's PR department, a PR firm, or a media release distribution service (examples on page 90).

Fact Sheet

After your press release itself, your fact sheet (factsheet or fact file) may be the most important item in your media kit.[20] The fact sheet concisely summarizes your organization and gives perspective to your news release to induce a journalist to write about the subject. Usually confined to one printed page, a fact sheet presents key points, using bullets, headings, tables, and other means to make it concise and easy to follow. A fact sheet may be a simple bulleted list focusing on numbers and statistics, like the example in Figure 2.8.

Fact sheets often contain answers to common questions (FAQs), educational facts, how-to advice, product information, statistics, and technical data. Sometimes fact sheets go beyond just the facts and develop an interesting story to engage the journalist. Infographics format is ideal for storytelling, as shown in Figure 2.9.

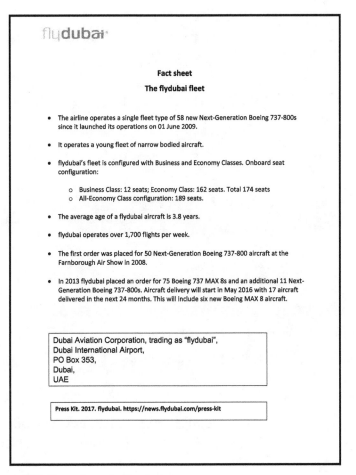

Figure 2.8 Fact sheet in list format

Source: Dubai Aviation Corporation, 2018. Used by permission.

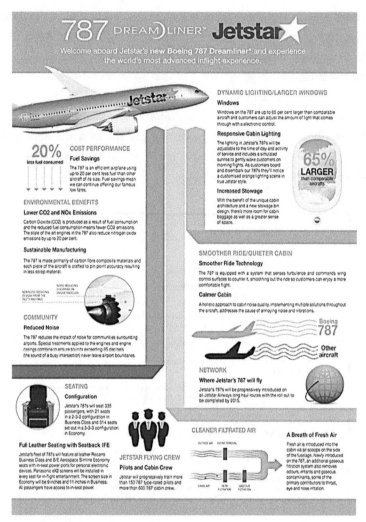

Figure 2.9 Fact sheet in infographic format

Source: Jetstar Airlines, 2018. Used by permission.

Backgrounder

A backgrounder, found in most business press kits, may summarize all important aspects of a company.[21] For example, it may include the following background information.

- Contributions to society and the industry
- History

- Organizational structure and capitalization (nonprofits include fundraising sources)
- Management team (board of directors of nonprofit organizations)
- Market, sales volume, and market position
- Mission statement
- Strengths
- Technologies

Alternatively, your backgrounder may focus on interesting points about the specific product, place, organization, issue, event, or controversy in your press release. A backgrounder expands on the press release it accompanies and helps keep that release extremely concise.

One important purpose of a backgrounder is to establish the accuracy of your press release information and the authenticity of your company, especially a new business or one entering a new market. Backgrounders also help journalists decide whether coverage of your company's news fits the media outlet's policies and purposes. An individual journalist reading your backgrounder has likely read your press release and is intrigued. Now he or she reads the backgrounder to answer two important questions.

- Is the press release information coming from a credible, solid source?
- Do I have enough information to create a news story?

Opinions vary on the appropriate length of a backgrounder: Some bloggers say it—like the press release—should be confined to one page. Others say a backgrounder may contain two or three pages, and one writer recommended four or five pages. Ideally, you will let your topic and available information determine the length rather than aiming for a specific page count.

Backgrounder Elements

Writers of media kit pieces often confuse backgrounders and fact sheets, including some of the same content in both documents. To avoid this error, think of a backgrounder as a narrative including five components.

- *Overview.* Backgrounders usually begin with a one-paragraph overview that often ties into the press release subject.
  The remaining components may appear in any order that seems appropriate to the writer and some may involve two or three paragraphs.
- *Scope.* This component describes who is affected by your press release's subject. The scope usually entails demographic or geographic data or both.
- *Objectives or Process.* This backgrounder component often refers to founding principles and involves an organization's mission statement or philosophy. Alternatively, this component may focus on organizational process—the way a company is organized, the way it operates, and key players (management team members) relevant to your story. *Note*: For well-written biography examples, visit the Softonic website (https://hello.softonic.com/press/#exec-bios), which contains a dozen bios of Softonic leaders and board of directors.
- *History.* This element describes the origins and major milestones of the whole company or the product, place, organization, issue, event, or controversy in the press release. History may be written as a single paragraph or as a timeline in list form. In any case, include historical highlights only.

  Previous press coverage may go a long way in establishing legitimacy of your organization. Therefore, consider listing news outlets that publicized your company in the past few years, along with each item's headline and any pull quotes (text from an article that also appears in a box and distinct font).
- *Conclusion.* The last paragraph may include the boilerplate information from your press release. At least give the location of the company's offices and plants, its Internet home page, and a separate media kit or newsroom web page if one exists.

Practically all backgrounders involve the five elements somehow, and occasionally a company backgrounder uses Scope, History, and so on as subheadings, as shown in Figure 2.10.

Notice the following features of Figure 2.10.

- Though not printed on Rain Bird Corporation letterhead, the heading clearly identifies the company, as well as contact information.
- The trademarked subheading under the company name adds perspective to this report.
- While Rain Bird Corporation's overview contains more than one paragraph, it omits reference to a specific news topic; but that information, if desired, could be inserted by each writer of a press release.

COMPANY BACKGROUNDER

Contact: Alex Nathanson
Corporate Marketing Brand Manager
(626) 812-3463
anathanson@rainbird.com

RAIN BIRD CORPORATION

The Intelligent Use of Water™

It is often one person's vision, fueled by passion and need that leads to innovation. So it was with Thomas Edison's light bulb, Alexander Graham Bell's telephone, Eli Whitney's cotton gin and Orton Englehart's impact sprinkler. Englehart, a Southern California citrus grower, revolutionized the food production industry and ushered in a new era in worldwide irrigation when he invented the horizontal action impact drive sprinkler in 1933.

Clem and Mary LaFetra, neighbors of the inventor, recognized the sprinkler's potential and began to market it. Soon after, they set up a manufacturing facility in the family barn and began production. They chose the company's name, Rain Bird, from an ancient Native American legend about a great bird that brought life-giving rain following a terrible drought.

Scope

Today, more than eight decades after its entrance into the market, Rain Bird Corporation is still a private company based in Azusa, California. The LaFetra family and their employees built the company into the largest manufacturer of irrigation systems in the world. Rain Bird offers over 4,000 water-saving irrigation products and services, meeting the diverse watering needs of homeowners, contractors, farmers, golf course superintendents and commercial property managers -- in over 130 countries.

While the company initially focused on irrigation of citrus crops, one of its first commercial customers in the early '30s was the Los Angeles Country Club. Today, Rain Bird irrigation products are used to efficiently water private homes, universities, golf courses, botanical gardens, resorts, sports arenas, amusement parks, orchards and vineyards throughout the United States and the world.

Worldwide soccer fans have marveled at the beautiful playing conditions at premier stadiums in South Africa and Brazil; golfers enjoy year-round tournament conditions at Pebble Beach Golf Links in California. Then there are the wonderful gardens at LEGOLAND® California maintained by a Rain Bird system designed for non-potable water; or the orchards and vineyards throughout the world that use Rain Bird A5PC Dripline to irrigate hundreds of acres of almonds and wine grapes; and the many beautiful botanic gardens and arboreta throughout the world that rely on Rain Bird systems to stay lush and healthy.

History

The original Rain Bird impact sprinkler, patented in 1935 (U.S. Patent #1,997,901), was designated a historic landmark of agricultural engineering in 1990. Over the years, Rain Bird has been awarded more than 450 patents for its innovative irrigation technology ranging from spray heads and nozzles to valves, rotors and central control systems. Recent examples include:

- XFS Subsurface Dripline, winner of the 2010 Irrigation Show Best New Product Award, which efficiently irrigates turf grass from below the surface.

-more-

Figure 2.10 Company backgrounder

Source: Rain Bird Corporation, 2018. Used by permission.

- Rain Curtain™ rotor nozzles and HE-VAN high efficiency spray nozzles that offer superior water distribution.
- In-stem pressure regulating sprinklers that eliminate misting and fogging to help save water.
- ESP-SMTe smart irrigation control system that brings advanced weather-based control to the home-
  owner level and reduces water use by up to 70%.
- SST irrigation timer that simplifies watering with revolutionary zone-based programming while including water saving features like automatic rain shut-off and one touch seasonal adjustment.

Rain Bird's Objectives and Organization

Since its inception, Rain Bird's commitment to quality has been unmatched in the industry. The company maintains a state-of-the-art product research and testing facility in Tucson, Arizona where products are routinely
tested under the most extreme conditions to ensure they perform reliably in the field, season after season.

Rain Bird's focus on the most efficient use of water can be found throughout Rain Bird's innovative products. It
also shows in its services, such as **Rain Bird's Sprinkler Design Service** for homeowners; in the **Rain Bird
Academy seminars and training programs** for landscape and irrigation professionals; and in **greener landscapes accompanied by lower water bills**. All of Rain Bird's products, whether used for farms, golf courses,
contractors, commercial or consumer landscapes, are **designed with two priorities in mind**: water conservation
and the environment. As the global industry leader of irrigation applications and services, Rain Bird's broad
range of irrigation products remain on the forefront of water-saving technology.

The company's commitment to The Intelligent Use of Water extends beyond its products and into public education campaigns, which include **a series of white papers and public service announcements**; and **membership
in the Alliance for Water Efficiency** and the **steering committee advising the U.S. Environmental Protection Agency (EPA)** on its WaterSense product labeling program. In 2015 Rain Bird launched the **"25 Ways to
Save 25%"** website (http://25ways.rainbird.com) to provide a resource to consumers on water-efficient irrigation options in response to the prolonged California drought. Rain Bird also has partnerships with nonprofit organizations, including sponsorship of water management education initiatives with the American Society of
Golf Course Architects (ASGCA) and the Landscape Architecture Foundation's Rain Bird Intelligent Use of
Water™ Scholarship, the Environmental Leaders in Golf Awards, and numerous product donations to organizations like Habitat for Humanity and the National Gardening Association's Youth Garden Grant.

Conclusion

Rain Bird has also received numerous awards for its commitment to environmental preservation, and was hon-
ored as the **R. Marlin Perkin's Conservation Organization of The Year** in **2003**. In **2014**, the European Irrigation Association (EIA) presented Rain Bird with the **Golf Gold Award** for the Rain Bird IC Integrated Control System. In **2015**, the National Business Research Institute (NBRI) recognized Rain Bird Corporation with
the **Circle of Excellence award**. In **2016**, Rain Bird received the **2016 Readers Choice Award** from Facility
Executive Magazine in the water management category.

Rain Bird has offices in more than 20 countries. The company maintains state-of-the-art manufacturing and assembly facilities in the United States, China and Mexico. For more information, visit Rain Bird's website at
http://www.rainbird.com.

#

Figure 2.10 (Continued)

- The use of bold font and bullets makes for easier and quicker
  reading.
- The backgrounder omits visuals. However, the Rain Bird
  Corporation website (address concludes the report) includes
  photographs, an infographic summarizing The Intelligent Use
  of Water™, and videos and podcasts for VNRs or SMNRs.
- The backgrounder does not reference past publicity because
  the company website includes all Rain Bird Corporation
  media releases dating to 2009.
- At the bottom of page 1, inclusion of the word more is
  essential. Likewise, at the bottom of page 2, inclusion of the
  hashmarks is vital to indicate the end of the backgrounder.

Backgrounder Writing Guides

Managers with backgrounder writing experience recommended these practices.[22]

- *If providing a printed backgrounder, print the first page on company letterhead*, with successive pages on plain paper.
- *Copy the contact information on your press release into the backgrounder.*
- *If your organization has a backgrounder that is used repeatedly, read it carefully to ensure it is up to date.* Fine-tune the standard backgrounder—especially the first paragraph—to incorporate a summary of the current press release subject. Then proceed to relate this information to your company's background.
- *Do not make backgrounders into advertisements or sales pitches.* Focus on engaging journalists' interest in your news story.
- *Insert subheadings in your report, making it easier to read and grasp.* Ideally each heading will summarize the text below it. Also use easy-to-reference graphics.
- *For all outside research mentioned in your backgrounder, cite sources in your report and provide a list of references.* Thus, journalists can verify your information, a common practice. To ensure consistency, follow an appropriate style guide, such as AP Style.[23]
- *Show consideration for the journalist by making ample information available.* For example, if you write about a new product, insert a URL linking reporters to a page showing complete product specifications, media mentions, and pricing.
- *Make sure your backgrounders are accurate*—even avoid rounding numbers. The media may print or air any inaccuracies you include. If you provided the information, getting a retraction would be nearly impossible.
- *For multiple uses, ensure that your backgrounders look equally good in print and on screen.* For example, it may be stored itally on the media pages of your organization's website and printed as a handout during a press event.

> - *Only include biographies of people who are relevant to the news you are releasing.* For example, for news highlighting your company's technological superiority, your backgrounder might include the biography (bio) of the company's research and development (R&D) director. In this instance, a bio of the organization's sales manager would not be helpful.
> - *Keep bios short (three paragraphs maximum).* Include only information directly related to your news. For example, in the R&D director's bio you would likely include the person's 11 years working for Google but omit the director's pets or favorite sports team.

Though writing PR reports may not be an on-the-job routine for you, you may want to keep up with activity in the PR field. These recommended websites will help you do so.[24]

- *Bad Pitch Blog* (www.badpitchblog.com). This blog helps a writer prevent typical PR blunders.
- *PR In Your Pajamas* (http://prinyourpajamas.com). This blog is ideal for a person just starting PR writing.
- *Ragan's PR Daily* (https://prdaily.com/Main/Home.aspx). This website continually offers tips for keeping up to date in the PR arena.
- *Spinsucks* (https://spinsucks.com). This site provides expert advice on a range of PR topics—from advertising and communication to search engine optimization (SEO) and social media.

The reports just discussed publicize, or promote, a company that uses them; and promotion is part of most organizations' marketing plan. However, the two reports shown in the following section are all-out marketing reports, designed to identify prospective customers or pin-down sales of specific products or services.

Marketing Reports

Even if you are not directly involved in planning and executing marketing and sales activities in your organization, you may be appointed to a team charged with publishing a white paper or preparing a business proposal. White papers educate readers (potential customers) about a company's area of expertise and can be useful for generating sales leads. Thus, white papers support an organization's overall marketing efforts. (*Note*: A 2015 study by Content Marketing Institute and Marketing Profs found that 68% of marketers used white papers.[25]) Business proposals lay out plans for meeting a reader's business need or solving a business problem. Thus, business proposals affect an organization's sales of goods and services.

White Papers

Traditional marketing involved pitching—using carefully planned presentation strategies to persuade consumers to buy products or services. Those traditional practices have given way to content marketing—creating and distributing valuable content (online material, such as blogs, e-mail newsletters, social media posts, and videos) that helps existing and prospective customers solve their business problems. Without promoting their brand, content marketers stimulate customer interest and demonstrate their companies' expertise. As a result, they draw and keep a well-defined audience, many of whom will make a purchase.[26]

White Papers Then and Now

As already noted, many marketers deliver content in reports called white papers to instruct potential customers on a single topic involving a product, service, solution, or technique the organization offers for sale. Since the 1920s, businesses have used white papers to teach future buyers. Except for an increase in color printing and illustration, white papers changed little over the decades—until about 20 years ago. Most contemporary white papers differ markedly from their forerunners.

- *Today's white papers contain fewer pages.* Traditionally, business white papers contained 15 to 30 or more (up to 50) pages. Current white papers typically contain 7 to 15 pages. Experts recommend a minimum of six pages for introducing, developing, and concluding a topic. The same experts note that in the modern, time-conscious business world, readers are likely to read (skim) for a maximum of, say, 5 to 10 minutes.

- *Businesses use different distribution methods.* Originally, white papers were printed on very high-quality paper and mailed to prospective customers—mostly other businesses. Today's white papers are PDF documents posted on companies' websites, accessible to business-to-business (B2B) and business-to-consumer (B2C) markets.

- *Today's white papers may have a different appearance.* Traditionally, white papers used plain, letter-sized (8.5 in. by 11 in.) pages, and many still do. These days, though, white papers often resemble a slide deck (16-in. by 12-in. pages).

  In the past, text-heavy pages filled these reports, with minimal blank space and few graphic elements and visuals to break the monotony. More recently, pages may contain extremely spare text and sophisticated graphics.

- *Today's white papers have fewer parts.* Because these marketing reports today tend to be shorter than their forerunners, they also tend to be less structured, resulting in fewer parts. Historically, most white papers contained the following elements; and some current ones contain vestiges of these parts.

  o Title page—opening page displaying the white paper's title and publisher.

  o Table of contents—list of section titles or descriptions, along with the beginning page number of each section.

  o Executive summary or Abstract—a 200-word (approximate) overview of the white paper, allowing readers to become aware of its content without having to read the entire document.

  o Introduction—opening paragraph(s) laying groundwork for understanding the main text. Points made here were expanded in the report body.

  o Report body—several pages of text outlining a common business problem, followed by several pages offering a solution and several more pages noting examples of results obtained using said solution. Occasional illustrations,

sidebars (columns of supplementary information), and
frequent subheadings helped offset large amounts of text.

o Conclusion—synthesis of information in the report body,
showing its importance to readers and propelling them to a
new understanding of the subject.

- *Today's white papers usually end with a call to action.* As you
know, a call to action consists of words carefully chosen to
motivate readers to respond quickly or purchase immediately.
A call to action example follows.[27]

Tableau helps people see and understand their data with drag-and-
drop analytics that anyone can use. Create and publish dashboards and
share them with colleagues, partners, or customers—no programming
skills required. Begin a free trial today.
TABLEAU.COM/TRIAL

- *The writing style, though, differs only slightly.* Today's successful
writers of white papers use a professional writing style, but
not extremely formal. Traditionally, though, these marketing
reports involved a formal writing style, marked by impersonal language. Currently, as in the past, white papers omit
the hype or puffery that are common in advertisements and
company brochures. The latter are usually ostentatious and
include recognizable sales pitches. A white paper also omits
opinions and unverified claims. Instead it is designed to persuade with facts and data that backup those facts.

Figure 2.11 shows excerpts from an 18-page white paper.[28] Notice the
smart graphics, page dimensions, and sparse text on this trendy example.

Figure 2.12 (pp. 107 and 108) also displays selections from an 18-page
white paper.[29]

In this example, notice that the report body includes active links to
various websites. Thus, readers can verify data cited in the white paper
and delve into it more deeply as they read.

Notice, also, that the arrow points to a citation of a publication. This
report contains five such notes, and a list of endnotes ends the white

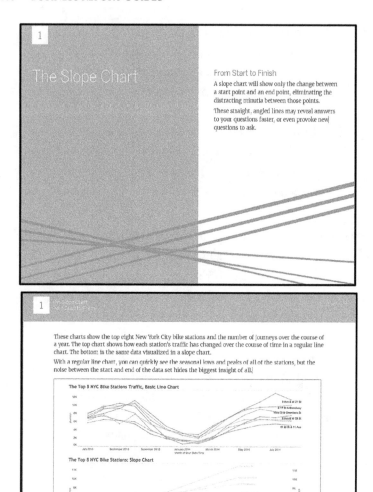

Figure 2.11 Pages of a white paper with slide-size pages, stylish graphics, and succinct text

Source: Tableaux Software, 2018. Used by permission.

paper. All cited titles are web documents, and links in the endnotes enables readers to navigate those sources easily.

In addition, notice the drop-in quotations in large print. Besides supplying pertinent information, they add visual interest to the pages.

For additional examples, see the diverse collection of 12 business white papers authored by Gordon Graham, That White Paper Guy.[30]

Figure 2.12 Pages of a white paper with drop-in quotations, embedded links, and source citations

Source: Hootsuite Inc. 2018. Used by permission.

In addition, the American Marketing Association's website includes a white papers library.[31]

White Paper Best Practices

Marketers who distribute them know the positive result that white papers can have on buying decisions. They also know that effective white papers require more time, effort, and dollars than most other forms of content. Therefore, anyone faced with creating a white paper or contributing to one needs to know what to do—and not do—to make it highly successful.

Figure 2.12 (Continued)

Guides to Planning a White Paper

- Answer these questions about the white paper before beginning to draft it.[32]
- *What is a realistic timeline for completing the white paper?* Experts agree that the time to prepare an effective white paper varies between a few weeks and a few months. Allow ample time for drafting, revising, editing, and designing it.
- *What white paper parts will you include?* Some experts insist on using an executive summary, introduction (points to be covered), and conclusion (summary of the most striking

points). Answer this question after considering the complexity of your content and the makeup of your competitors' white papers.

- *How will you make people aware of the white paper?* Promotional options are many, including separate page of the company website, company blog with an overview of it, e-mail newsletter, online press release, social media (especially Google+, LinkedIn, and Twitter). Another often-used option: a landing page (usually a standalone web page from which the white paper can be downloaded). Using a combination of options will maximize exposure.

- *Will you gate the white paper or distribute it ungated?* That is, will you require some input in exchange for access to the downloadable white paper? Gating is not essential for generating sales leads with a white paper, but most companies do collect at least an e-mail address for each download.

- *If the white paper is gated, what data will you request in exchange for access to it?* Ask for the data you will need to do an initial follow up of your leads—no more. Users may be put off by a request for much detailed information and the time involved to provide it. Besides an e-mail address, many companies ask for first and last name and phone number. In Figure 2.13 Oracle's landing page asks for more data than usual for a gated white paper.

Besides an e-mail address, this landing page requests first and last name, company name, job title, ZIP code, country, company revenue, and industry.

Guides for Creating White Paper Content

Readers of white papers rightfully expect high-quality content—information that is easy to read, understand, and remember. Therefore, white paper writers must build in all the characteristics of effective reports described in Chapter 1, under Planning a Narrative Report (p. 6). The following list highlights other actions to take and some to avoid.[33]

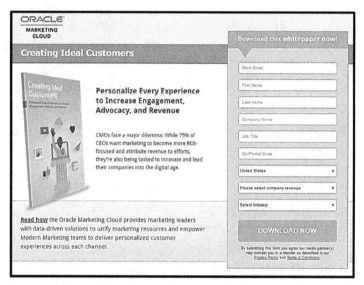

Figure 2.13 White paper landing page

Source: Oracle Marketing Cloud. 2018. Used by permission granted at https://oracle.com/legal/copyright.html

- *Plan content carefully.* Know who you are writing for, the business problems they face, and the kinds of information they need from your company. Of course, you want to address their most important problems. At the same time, you must focus on subjects in which your organization excels.
- *Consider whether a case study or an e-book would be more appropriate* than a white paper. In a case study you would summarize how your product ... helped one well-known customer. An e-book, longer than a white paper and often less formal, would be a good choice to cover a broad topic.
- *Prepare a written outline of the content.*[34] Plan sidebars, too.
  o If your white paper is relatively short and straightforward, an informal outline will likely do. An informal outline—a tool for generating ideas and organizing them—is a list of topics (words, short phrases, or a combination) to be included in the report. A handy way to prepare an informal outline includes three steps.

1. List topics to be included in the white paper.
2. Edit the topic list to be sure it contains all essential topics and no unnecessary information.
3. Arrange topics in a sequence that shows relationships of key points and satisfies the communication needs of your readers.

o For a complex situation, you may be dealing with a considerable amount of data and an extensive analysis of that data. To produce a coherent, well-organized report in that case, prepare a formal outline, involving (a) structured numbering system to show the various levels into which the report is divided and (b) phrases or sentences to describe the content of each division and subdivision of the report.

The traditional outline system consists of Roman numerals to indicate first-level divisions, uppercase letters for second-level divisions, Arabic numerals for third-level divisions, and lowercase letters for fourth-level divisions. Few outlines progress beyond fourth-level divisions; but when you need such divisions, continue the numbering system by alternating Arabic numerals and lowercase letters.

The following outlining guides will help you outline effectively.

- *Give every division and subdivision at least two parts.* Logically, nothing can be divided into fewer than two parts. Therefore, every topic that is divided must have a minimum of two subtopics.

- *Balance the divisions.* All divisions need not have the same number of topics and subtopics; but if any section of your outline is considerably longer or shorter than other sections, you should reevaluate the outline. Lack of balance may suggest the need to regroup information for a more coherent report structure.

- *Help readers focus quickly on significant report content.* When any part of an outline contains more than

four division levels, you may be focusing the reader's
attention on minor rather than major points.

- *State division headings concisely.* Topic headings (one
  word or a short phrase that names the subject of the
  following content) may be too concise to communicate report content to readers. Talking headings
  (concise, newspaper-style headers) provide more
  information about the white paper content. Lengthy
  talking headings, however, may distract.

- *Write division headings in parallel form; that is, the
  same grammatical structure.* Make first-level headings
  parallel. Make second-level headings parallel within
  that division, too, but not necessarily parallel with
  other levels. For example, you might express all
  first-level headings as questions and all second-level
  headings as statements and third-level headings as
  clauses, phrases, or keywords.

- *Special timesaving tools in most word processing software help you create and reorganize outlines,* as well
  as evaluate the organization of a finished report. In
  Microsoft Word 365, for example, both the multi-
  level-list tool and the outline view are designed to
  facilitate outlining. Outline view is the more versatile
  of the two, in that you can quickly change the level
  and order of topics, as well as reduce visual clutter by
  hiding selected parts of an outline.

- *Use an engaging title (headline).* Make up a working title
  before drafting the white paper. When revising content,
  carefully consider the need to revise the title as well. Get
  attention and pique interest by establishing a clear benefit
  to readers in the headline. Give the title a professional
  tone, avoid one that suggests entertainment. Ensure
  that you can fulfill the expectation your headline sets.
  In Figure 2.12, for example, the title "8 Tips for Building
  a Social Business" meant the content writer needed to
  include eight distinct and equally developed tips.

- *If used, condense the table of contents, abstract, and introduction.* Readers are looking for information they can apply immediately. Do not withhold that information.
- *Answer specific questions.* Know what information customers look for from you and give it to them. Doing so may require a brief e-mail survey of current customers, a short online survey of website visitors, or some other method of gathering insight into what current and future customers expect from your company.
- *Write concisely, but do not limit text and pages too drastically.* Gordon Graham, renowned for authoring white papers, related an experiment in which he attempted—rather unsuccessfully—to develop two- and three-page white papers. So, think of six pages as an absolute minimum for a successful white paper.
- *Deliver factual content based on research.* Take advantage of your research options.
  o Read the prominent research reports in your industry. Examples follow.[35]
    - *Annual Reports* (www.annualreports.com)—access 53,000 annual reports from 5,100 companies worldwide
    - *Corporate Affiliations*™ (http://corporateaffiliations.com/default/index?id=routetohome)—search nearly two million company profiles and over three million decision-makers
    - *Corporate Information* (www.corporateinformation.com)—offers analytical reports on 39,000 companies from 85 countries
    - *Kompass* (http://us.kompass.com)—search for business tools and solutions across five million selected company profiles in more than 60 countries
    - *Public Register Online, The* (www.annualreportservice.com)—view or request hard copy of 5,000 online annual reports or 10-K presentations (annual report

of financial condition presented to Security and
Exchange Commission on Form 10-K)

- *WallStreet Research*™ (www.wallstreetresearch.org)—
corporate profiles, newsletters, and detailed research
reports on emerging companies

o In addition, read relevant reports at government websites, such as the following.[36]

- *Catalog of U.S. Government Publications*, or CGP
(https://catalog.gpo.gov/F?RN=319705784)—electronic and print publications from executive, judicial,
and legislative branches of U.S. government

- *E-Commerce Statistics*, or E-STATS (www.census.
gov/programs-surveys/e-stats.html)—measures the
electronic economy

- *FedStats* (https://fedstats.sites.usa.gov)—data and
trends from 100 federal agencies on a wide array of
business-related topics

- *U.S. Government Publishing Office*, or GPO, Economic Indicators (www.gpo.gov/fdsys/browse/col-
lection.action?collectionCode=ECONI)—economic
information on a vast range of business activity

- *Small Business Administration*, or SBA (www.sba.
gov)—articles and resources for starting and managing a small business

- *United States Patent and Trademark Office*, or USPTO
(www.uspto.gov)—general information about patents, intellectual property, and trademarks

o Consider engaging a research consulting group to conduct the primary research for your company. Four of the
best-known research consulting firms:

- Forrester (https://go.forrester.com)
- Gartner (https://gartner.com)
- IDC (https://idc.com/about)
- Thomson Reuters (https://thomsonreuters.com/en.html).

- o For results not available to your competitors, conduct original research. Outcomes of your own primary research establish your organization as an authority and give you something unique. In addition, you will learn about your customer base and industry in the process of collecting primary data (data acquired at their source by means of company records, experimentation, focus group and individual interviews, observation, and questionnaire surveys).
- *Display data in charts, graphs, maps, and tables*, which allow the data to be read extremely rapidly and memorably. Stay current on data visualization techniques.
- *Plan images from the outset and while drafting the text.* Besides data displays and other visual enhancements, including bullets, pull quotes, and shaded text boxes, well-chosen photographs can also convey information.
- *To connect with today's productivity conscious audience, include video in your white paper as reinforcement.* Use short video clips—under five minutes if just one or under two minutes per report section.
- *Revise and edit your initial draft.* Select a reader-reviewer in advance and arrange revising and editing procedures that are efficient for both of you, such as the track changes feature in Google Docs or Microsoft Word.
  - o Revise content first. Does the draft answer the readers' likely questions? Is any important information missing? Is all information factual? Double-check all facts, stats, and data sources. Check the report for jargon and any examples of sales hype.
  - o Edit language mechanics extremely carefully, keeping in mind that the white paper may represent your company in various ways for a year or more. See the editing tips in Appendix A (p. 195).

Guides for Designing a White Paper

Assume that readers of your white paper will expect a visual masterpiece in addition to high-quality content. Therefore, whenever you begin planning content, start imagining the white paper's appearance.[37]

Use design to enhance content. The design must never distract, present obstacles, or call attention to itself. The design should help readers by adding clarity. Design entails page layout, images, fonts, and colors. Even if you hire a designer rather than designing it yourself, be prepared to tell the designer what you have in mind. Achieve your visual masterpiece using the following design guides.

- *Make all margins—top, bottom, left, and right—at least one inch.* Never disrupt margin settings to squeeze in additional text.
- *If your white paper is long, use a two-column format (see Figure 2.12).* The shorter lines enable faster reading and skimming.
- *Use a ragged (slightly uneven) right margin.* Leave hyphenation off. If the margin becomes too ragged, insert a manual hyphen at the line ending to divide a long word (seven or more letters) between syllables.
- *Do not start a new section within a line or two of the bottom margin.* Instead leave blank space and move the new section heading to the next page. Ideally, each new section begins on a new page. Intermittent blank spaces allow a reader's eyes to rest.
  - *Keep the number of visuals small enough that each stands out*—generally two or three visuals on an 8.5-in. by 11-in. page.
  - *Take photos using a digital camera,* rather than your phone or tablet. Set the camera for the largest picture size and highest resolution. Most photographs should be action shots of a person or several people—mainly customers and staff. Stand close to the photo subject(s) so that they fill the frame.

- o *Using stock photos is also acceptable.* Choose shots showing people performing tasks related to your white paper
  topic. As a rule, include a photo caption.
- o *When a photo is too large for the space, cut (crop) unnecessary parts* from the visual. If the photo cannot be
  cropped, resize, or scale, it in both height and width (the
  aspect ratio).
- o *Consider eye movement when placing photos.* A profile
  photograph of a person should be placed so that the
  person is looking into the page rather than off the side
  of the page.
- o *Touch-up your photos with image-editing software* before
  inserting them into your layout. Adjust the brightness,
  color, contrast, and so on to prevent a murky appearance. Examples include:
  - Gimp (www.gimp.org)
  - Pixlr (pixlr.com)
  - PhotoScape (www.photoscape.org/ps/main/index.
    php) and PhotoScape X for Mac (x.photoscape.org/
    mac)
  - SumoPaint (www.sumopaint.com/home)
- *Use a size 12 font for the paragraphs.* Size 10 is adequate
  for notes. Use a display size (15 and up) for headings and
  pull quotes.
- *Consider posting two versions of each white paper:* one for
  reading on screen that uses a sans serif font for paragraphs
  and one that uses a serif font for the many individuals who
  prefer to print white papers and read from hard copy.
- Strictly limit the use of ALL CAPS, bold style, italics style,
  and underlining. Add emphasis with bullet points (when
  order of list items is irrelevant), numbered items (when
  sequence or ranking matters), and shaded text.
- *Ensure sharp contrast between the text and background.* For
  sharpness, nothing works better than black characters on a
  white ground. Generally, vision changes occur around age

> 40; and most decision makers who read white papers are over 40.
>
> - If no one involved in creating your white paper is a skilled designer, consider hiring one and providing direction. You may begin with an online search for freelancers who create white papers or go to the Upwork (https://upwork.com) website to select a freelance graphic designer who specializes in white papers. In addition, here are the names of organizations that write and design white papers.
>   o ArtVersion (https://artversion.com)
>   o Richard Goulde Writing (https://richardgoulde.com)
>   o That White Paper Guy (https://thatwhitepaperguy.com)

Since white papers support an organization's overall marketing efforts, you will do well to follow these best practices.

Business Proposals

A proposal offers a plan of action. The objective of a proposal is to influence others—to persuade someone to act in a way that the proposer considers good or desirable. Business proposals share that general purpose, even though they have many different specific purposes.

Purposes of Proposals

A proposal may be solicited or unsolicited. A solicited proposal is presented in response to a request for proposal (often abbreviated RFP). In the RFP, the requesting person or agency indicates its needs, and the proposal writer attempts to show that the proposed action can satisfy those needs. *Note*: When sending RFPs, companies naturally send identical requests to several likely providers. Thus, proposal writing in some cases becomes a highly competitive undertaking.

An unsolicited proposal is initiated by the proposer. That individual perceives a need or problem and offers a research plan, a product or service, or an action to satisfy the need. The proposal may be submitted to someone who is unaware of the situation. The writer's purpose is twofold: (1) to convince the reader that a need or problem exists and (2) to show how the proposed action will result in benefits to the reader.

Kinds of Proposals

Business proposals fall into three categories: (1) proposals to provide a product or service; (2) proposals to change a policy, procedure, or organizational structure; and (3) proposals to investigate or conduct research. Each may be independent of the others, but the three may also be related to one another. For example, assume that as a human resources director you recognize that rising worker-compensation costs require the company to find alternatives to losing trained employees who have been injured on the job. You first write a proposal to investigate the feasibility of implementing a rehabilitation program for injured employees. Upon receiving approval for the proposed research, you ask one of your associates to conduct the research. Perhaps the research plan calls for a survey of employees to determine their attitudes about rehabilitating injured employees and integrating them into the work force. You decide that you want an external agency to conduct that employee survey, and you request that a professional testing agency submit a proposal to provide that service. If the completed research shows that an employee rehabilitation program is a cost-effective way of returning injured employees to the workplace, you will write an operational proposal to management recommending immediate adoption of such a program.

Service Proposals

Service or product proposals (sometimes called bids) offer to provide something for the recipient. Such proposals are often solicited. The RFP frequently specifies the exact content and format desired by the receiver. To increase the probability that your proposal will be considered, you must adhere to those specifications.

Some organizations use relatively informal procedures to solicit product or service proposals. For example, a training director may call a consultant, describe a training need, and ask for a proposal. In such a situation, the consultant chooses the proposal's content and structure. Both must convince the training director that the consultant understands the need and can satisfy it. Figure 2.14 demonstrates a service proposal.

Notice that the service proposal includes five things the reader requires for an informed decision.

- General description of the reader's problem or needs
- Description of the service the writer can provide

C–J COMMUNICATION ASSOCIATES

859 River Drive
Iowa City, IA 54441

phone: 319-555-4961
web: c-jcommunix.com

February 15, 2019

Ms. J. B. McCarthy, President
Board of Directors
Iowa Optometric Association
158 Hawkeye Boulevard
Iowa City, IA 52240

Dear Ms. McCarthy

In response to your February 12 phone request, I submit this proposal for a study of communication between and among members of the Board of Directors of the Iowa Optometric Association.

Background

My understanding is that the Board of Directors of the Iowa Optometric Association wishes to improve communication among members during and between your monthly board meetings. You have been authorized by your board to solicit proposals for a study of the communication policies and procedures currently in use among board members. Your goal is to improve communication practices and thereby improve the board's productivity.

Procedure

I propose to follow these steps to fulfill your request:

1. Attend your board meeting in March to observe communication practices and interactions among board members during the meeting.

2. Review the Association's constitution, bylaws, and board manual to identify current communication expectations and guides that exist and to suggest improvements needed, if any.

3. Design a questionnaire to assess attitudes of board members about current communication practices between and among board members. You will be given the opportunity to review the questionnaire, and I will test it in an independent focus group before it is distributed to your board members.

4. Administer the questionnaire to your employees electronically. Board members will be sent an e-mail containing a link to the questionnaire, which they will complete online. I am the only person who will have access to the completed questionnaires.

Figure 2.14 Service proposal

Ms. J. B. McCarthy   -2-   February 15, 2019

5. Analyze and interpret all data obtained.

6. Present to you a written report containing the findings and recommendations resulting from the study.

7. Give an oral briefing to your Board on a date to be determined.

Cost

The cost for this service will be $4,000. I request an initial payment of $2,000 upon acceptance of this proposal; the final payment of $2,000 will be due upon completion of the report.

Completion Date

The final report will be presented to you no later than April 30. Completion by this date will allow you to institute any changes that may seem necessary as soon as the new board members take office in July. The following table shows my interim goals.

March 15	Attend meeting of Board of Directors to observe interactions
March 15–April 1	Analyze current constitution, bylaws, and board manual
April 1–5	Prepare, test, review, and upload questionnaires
April 8–12	Board members complete on-line questionnaire
April 13–18	Analyze all data
April 19–20	Complete and deliver report
May ?	Give oral briefing at monthly meeting of the Board of Directors

Qualifications

You indicated that you were referred to me by a client who had used my services in a similar situation. References of other satisfied clients will be provided at your request.

Request for Approval

Please call me if you have any questions about this proposal. Your approval before February 28 will ensure completion of the study in accordance with your plans for board development.

Sincerely

Carlota Flores

Carlota Flores, Communication Facilitator

Figure 2.14 Service proposal

- Cost of the proposed service
- Proposed completion date
- Qualifications of the service provider

Notice also that the proposal requests a specific action: the approval to proceed.

Operational Proposals

Operational or organizational proposals set forth a plan for changes in operations or organizational structure and provide objective information to justify the plan. Thus, operational proposals are like justification reports. This kind of proposal is often accompanied by an oral presentation containing more of the detailed data that make up the justification.

An example of an operational proposal appears in Figure 2.15.

Notice that the report structure and content complement the needs of busy executive committee members.

- Direct, clear statement of the proposed action
- Easy-to-read justification for that action
- Clear, concrete restatement of the desired action in closing

Research Proposals

The objective of a research proposal is to persuade the recipient to authorize the time and money required to carry out a significant research project.

Figure 2.15 Operational proposal

The persuasiveness of the proposal will depend on your ability to show that you understand the problem and have the knowledge and skills to conduct the study. Additional persuasive elements are honest, realistic estimates of time and resources needed for the project and evidence that you have considered how you will present your results. Before attempting to draft a research proposal, do careful preparation in 12 areas.[38] See Figure 2.16.

Proposal Content

As you prepare a research proposal, use this list of 12 planning areas as a guide. Include all parts that are relevant to the proposed study. The situation may justify omission of certain parts. For example,

Planning a Research Proposal	
Authorization	Are you approved to spend time and money on the research? Obtain or review your authorization.
Audience	Who will receive your research results—both the primary and secondary audiences? Identify your audience.
Research problem	Go beyond the managerial problem and its symptoms to the bigger picture. Define the research problem; put it in question form to help clarify.
Purpose	What do you hope to accomplish by doing the study? Clarify the purpose of the research. If you can, separate the purpose from the problem.
Scope	You may not be able to study all parts of the research problem; so, ask, which parts will lead me to useful facts? Narrow the scope of the problem.
Delimitations and limitations	What boundaries are you drawing between what you will and will not study? This question refers to delimitations. Could any practical limits on your research lower its applicability to the problem? This question refers to shortcomings or inadequacies due to circumstances beyond your control. State and explain your delimitations and potential limitations of the research.
Data collection	What kinds of information will you need to answer the research question? Should you use primary data (collected from records and/or people), secondary data (collected and published by others), or both? Plan for data collection.
Data analysis	Does the context call for qualitative or quantitative data? If the latter, then determine what statistical test to apply to the data you will collect. Plan for data analysis.
Time schedule	Plan backward from the due date, setting interim dates for completing each phase of the research. Estimate the time schedule.

Figure 2.16 *Plans contained in a research proposal*

Resources	Include realistic estimates of equipment, labor, supplies, travel, and other costs. Estimate all resources needed.
Results presentation	What will be the nature of your research report? What communication medium will you use to make your findings, conclusions, and recommendations known? Plan the presentation of results.
Approval	Present your research plan in person, in writing, or both and seek feedback. In most instances, you will want a contractual agreement before continuing with the project. Ask for approval to proceed.

Figure 2.16 (Continued)

stating delimitations or limitations is not necessary if the scope of the project is already stated very narrowly and no obvious limitations are foreseen.

In contrast, you may want to add specific information to increase the persuasiveness and thoroughness of your proposal. For example, the decision to narrow the scope—that is, include some elements and exclude others—implies a judgment that one route of analysis will lead to better results than another. Such a decision is an ethical judgment. Discussing a research problem with a group of colleagues who can judge the work impartially may help you identify the best set of factors to include in the scope. Then include a summary of that discussion in your proposal. Thus, you show the readers you thought through the problem, and you enable them to follow your reasoning.

Regarding data collection, if primary data are to be used in the research, the researcher and the person who authorizes the research have an ethical obligation to protect the confidentiality of the data and the safety of human and nonhuman subjects. In your proposal, explain the specific techniques you will use to protect confidentiality or provide safety or both.

The request for approval is more than a request for authorization of funds. Do you have (or can you acquire) the skills needed to carry out the research as proposed? Conversely, the person who gives approval has an ethical responsibility to evaluate the quality of the proposed research, its value to the organization, and the competence of those who will conduct the research. For that reason, include the qualifications of the person or team who will conduct the study to demonstrate competence to fulfill the proposal. Information of this type usually appears in an appendix with a reference to it in the proposal's request for approval section.

The order in which the parts are presented must contribute to the reader's understanding of what you plan to study. The presentation sequence should also lead the reader to appreciate the significance of the research. Since a research proposal is a complex document, structural devices such as headings, numbering, and tables can be used advantageously, as Figures 2.17a-d demonstrate.

SC State Ports Authority

Memo

To	Bryant T. Joseph, VP, Terminal Development
From	Melvin L Barbara, VP, Government Relations
Date	01/12/2020
Subject	Citizens' Attitudes toward Cruise Traffic

Background and Authorization

Recent letters to the editor in the *Charleston News and Courier* have indicated mixed attitudes about the docking of cruise ships at Union Pier in the Port of Charleston. For approximately 25 years, the Port of Charleston has been the site of one to three ship departures and arrivals per week. Currently this port serves as a home port and port of call for Carnival Cruise Lines as well as a port of call for other cruise lines. Home porting and port-of-call stops generally do not occur on the same days, except when emergencies, weather conditions, or other nautical events necessitate such multiple dockings. Although some merchants appreciate the increased business associated with the cruise dockings, other merchants and many local residents complain that the increased pedestrian and auto traffic distract from the traditional charm of Charleston. Discussions have been underway to move the cruise port to a different location along the Charleston Harbor waterfront in an attempt to alleviate some of the negative aspects of the departure and arrival of cruise ships.

At our management meeting on January 7 we discussed the need to determine objectively how the citizens of Charleston feel about the effects of cruise dockings in the Port of Charleston. We decided it was necessary to know more about those attitudes before launching a major study of the feasibility to relocate the cruise port. You asked me to design a study to explore those feelings.

Statement of the Problem

The objective of the study is to determine Charlestonians' perceptions of the economic and social impact of cruise dockings in the Port of Charleston and the possible relocation of the cruise terminal.

Purpose of the Study

The purpose of this study is to assess the business and social climate in which the Ports Authority will operate if it continues with plans to relocate the cruise terminal. Knowledge of that climate will help the Authority develop operational and communication strategies relative to the potential relocation.

Figure 2.17a Research proposal (authorization, problem, and purpose)

Bryant T. Joseph   2   01/12/2020

Scope of Analysis

Three factors will be studied:

1. What business impacts do the Charleston's downtown residents and merchants perceive to be related to the arrival and departure of cruise ships?

2. What personal and community impacts do Charleston's downtown residents and merchants perceive to be related to the arrival and departure of cruise ships?

3. What knowledge of and attitudes toward relocation of the cruise port are evidenced by Charleston's downtown residents and merchants?

Definitions

For purposes of this study, *residents* is used to designate persons living in the Ansonborough section of Charleston. The term *merchants* includes all commercial and professional units within the designated geographical area.

Delimitations

Because cruise passengers primarily frequent the area between the Charleston Harbor and King Street, the sample for this study will be drawn from merchants and residents in an area bounded by East Bay St. on the east, Broad St. on the south, King St. on the west, and Calhoun St. on the north. The sample of residents will be drawn from the Ansonborough district, which is located within those street boundaries.

The study period will be the months of June and August, confined to two days following the departure of a homeport ship and two days following the arrival and departure of a port-of-call ship. Ships will be selected from published cruise schedules, with ships departing at least three days from one another.

Limitations

The data collected will not represent attitudes of the business community or residents outside the downtown area, some of whom may also be affected by the cruise business. However, since the downtown community absorbs the major impact of the presence of cruise ships, the attitudes of that community can best direct decisions related to relocating the cruise port.

Since the data will be collected during the summer cruise season, the attitudes expressed may differ from attitudes expressed during an earlier or later cruise season. Nonetheless, the responses should be representative of attitudes developed during a peak tourist season in Charleston.

Methodology

This study will be based solely on primary data gathered by questionnaires completed by members of the target populations.

The sample. All merchants and residents within the defined geographical area will be invited to participate in the study

Figure 2.17b Research proposal (scope, definitions, delimitations and limitations, and description of data)

A research proposal is meant to persuade its recipient to approve a research project and commit the time and funds necessary to do it. Therefore, Figure 2.17 demonstrates the nine-step persuasive writing strategy discussed earlier (p. 79–81).

Proposal Approval

The person who receives a proposal from you may send you an e-mail, letter, or memo indicating approval and stating what the next step(s) will

Bryant T. Joseph   3   01/12/2020

Data collection. The data will be collected in two ways:

1. A letter will be mailed to all merchants inviting them to log onto a specified website on specified dates and complete an electronic questionnaire. The dates will be based on the docking of selected ships.
2. An invitation to attend a town-hall meeting will be mailed to all residential addresses in the Ansonborough district. The meetings will be scheduled to correspond to dockings of selected ships. At each meeting, the purpose of the study will be explained, attendees will be permitted to ask questions, and they will be asked to complete the questionnaire before leaving the meeting.

Data analysis. My staff will code the data obtained from the questionnaires and enter then into a statistical program. Summary statistics will be computed and interpreted.

Time Required

I propose the following schedule:

March	Design, test, and revise questionnaires; test data analysis program
April	Prepare letters to be sent to merchants and residents
May 1-May 15	Prepare and distribute a series of three news releases (newspaper, radio and television) to inform the community about the upcoming survey and encourage participation
May 15-May 30	Mail letters to merchants and half of Ansonborough residential addresses
June 1-5	Send reminder to attend town hall meeting
June 12 & 13	Conduct town-hall meetings following June 1 departure of Carnival cruise ship
June 15 & 16	Conduct town-hall meetings following June 15 port-of-call docking of Carnival cruise ship
June 17-July 30	Begin data entry and analysis regarding June dockings
August 1-5	Mail letters to remaining half of Ansonborough residents; mail reminders to merchants
August 14 & 15	Conduct town-hall meetings following August 13 departure of Carnival cruise ship
August 23 & 24	Conduct town-hall meetings following August 22 port-of-call docking of Carnival cruise ship
September 1-15	Complete data entry and analysis
September 20	Distribute completed written report to management committee
September 22	Discuss report with management during regular meeting

Figure 2.17c Research proposal (data collection and analysis and schedule)

be, leading to a formal contract. You could save time and effort, though, by using electronic signature technology to, in effect, turn your proposal into a signed contract.

For relatively short, simple proposals involving comparatively few resources, you might insert spaces for an electronic signature, or e-signature, at the end of the proposal itself. In high-stakes situations, you might include a formal contract—sanctioned by your organization's legal counsel—in an appendix, with spaces for one or more e-signatures. To do this, you would

Bryant T. Joseph   4   01/12/2020

Resources Needed

All research will be conducted by staff of the Government Affairs Division as part of our normal duties. We will use approximately 100 employee hours to prepare the data collection instruments, enter and analyze the data, and prepare the final report. We anticipate spending approximately 24 employee hours conducting the town-hall meetings. Standard cost allocations for respective grades will be applied. In addition, the project will incur direct costs for printing, supplies, postage, and town-hall meetings. The total project budget is $5,750:

Staff Labor	$3,750
Printing and supplies	750
Postage	750
Meeting expenses	500
Total	$5,750

Presentation of Results

I will present our findings, conclusions, and recommendations to the management committee in a formal written report prior to our September 20 management meeting and will be prepared to discuss the report at that meeting.

Request for Approval

Approval of this proposal by January 20 will permit the Government Affairs division to work this project into our schedule and adhere to the proposed schedule given in this proposal. If you have any questions in the meantime, please e-mail me (bryant.joseph@scspa.com).

Figure 2.17d Research proposal (resources, presentation, and approval)

upload your proposal file to an online signing service and mark or tag it where you want signatures to appear.[39] The signing service would then e-mail this marked-up file to whomever you specify. A receiver of the tagged file could sign it using the options available. For example:

- Type his or her name and select from various fonts to make the name look like an authentic signature.
- Draw the signature using a computer mouse or touchpad.
- Take a photo on a smart phone of his or her signature and upload it.
- Draw the signature with a finger on a mobile device that has the e-sign application installed.

The numerous online e-signing services vary in ease of use, features, pricing, and how they prove the validity of e-signatures over time. Therefore, the choice of an e-signing service requires study. A few reputable examples include the following.[40]

E-signing services:

- Adobe Document Cloud (formerly EchoSign) (acrobat. adobe.com)
- DocuSign (www.docusign.com)
- Eversign (https://eversign.com)
- RightSignature (rightsignature.com)
- Sertifi (www.sertifi.com)

E-signing is a means of expediting proposals. Approving a proposal by e-signing it makes it a legally binding contract, just as would a handwritten signature.

Summation Reports

Other nonroutine reports that you may be required to prepare include an abstract, an overview, and an executive summary. All three report types are summaries, and you may hear the terms used interchangeably. However, the following discussion emphasizes subtle differences in these reports.

Abstract

An abstract is text about a text—an abridgement of an entire published work. In the business world, abstracts are used to help managers keep up with current trends or issues in the industry. For example, assume your CEO skims each issue of *Academy of Management Journal.* In the latest issue, her attention was drawn to a 70-page research article of special interest. Her current schedule does not include the time needed for close reading and assimilation of the article. Thus, you may be asked to read the article and write a condensed version.

An abstract has the following attributes.[41]

- Introduces new information in each sentence.
- Follows the sequence of the text being summarized.
- Contains at least one sentence about each section of the text but omits all minor details.

- Involves impersonal, or third-person, language.
- Omits the abstract writer's interpretations and opinions.
- Includes title of the publication in the subject line or report title.
- Includes summary subheadings if the abstract exceeds one page.
- Emphasizes the author's conclusions and recommendations (if any).
- Includes in-text citations when the author is quoted along with complete references in a recognized documentation style, such as American Psychological Association (APA).[42]

Article abstracts may be viewed in *Harvard Business Review* online (https://hbr.org/magazine). Choose a magazine issue; display the table of contents; then view abstracts, which the publisher calls executive summaries.

Overview

Overviews, too, are used to help managers keep up with current trends or issues in their fields. An overview is a capsule, or very succinct review, of a single subject. Two examples highlight the importance of overview reports.

Example:

Senior officers need to stay abreast of business trends and issues in their specific industries. You may be asked to search various web sources and several professional or trade journals and write an overview of what you learn about a specific trend.

Example:

Your state legislature may be proposing more stringent pollution-control requirements. Upper management in your company needs an analysis of the proposed legislation and its potential impact on your company. You may be asked to study the issue in various ways and then prepare an overview.

An overview has the following characteristics.[43]

- Covers the *who*, *what*, *when*, and *where* questions of the subject; touches on the *why* and *how* questions.
- Uses headings and subheadings to show how the report is organized and how topics interrelate.
- Includes charts, graphs, maps, photos, and tables to aid clarity and conciseness.
- Integrates information from the various sources.
- Includes the report writer's interpretation and synthesis of information.
- Often shows conclusions and recommended actions.
- Includes a glossary if the subject involves technical terms.
- Often includes a keywords list, facilitating future study of the subject.

These characteristics—except the final two—can be observed in Figure 2.18 (pp. 134–37).

Cavort Sportwear

To: Aadi Newar

From: Jong Park

Date: April 13, 2019

Subject: Data Viz Studies

As you requested, I have summarized publications about the use of visuals to convey data in the company's print materials and web content. My reading uncovered some points for possible follow up, and my note and summary highlight these points.

Visuals serve important purposes in communicating data, but only if an appropriate graphic is used. Knowing the characteristics of various graphics is vital. Our eyes and mind evaluate graphical cues with different degrees of accuracy (Valiela, 2001). Studies show that the colors used in a graphic display can affect the time required to read it (Lin and Heer, 2014).

Graphic Cues and Perceptual Accuracy

In a classic study, William Cleveland asked participants to make judgments involving different visual cues. Using results of these experiments, along with other information, Cleveland ranked the cues from most accurate to least accurate for perceiving data, as shown in the following list (Valiela, 2001).

- Position along axis

- Length

- Angle or slope

- Area

- Volume

- Color or shade

Later, Jeffrey Heer, a data visualization expert, led a similar study and drew similar conclusions. Specifically, Heer's team ranked eight data encodings from most accurate to least accurate, as shown in the following list (Heer, 2015).

- Position on a common scale

- Position on a nonaligned scale

- Length

- Slope

- Angle

- Area

- Volume

- Color or shade

Figure 2.18 Overview of a topic (data visualization)

Aadi Newar   2   April 13, 2019

The results of Cleveland's study as well as Heer's findings indicate that readers will decode our graphs most accurately when we use bar graphs and line graphs, which involve data points on an axis or two, bars of varying lengths on a common baseline, or lines that form angles or slopes as they rise and fall. *Note:* Of 36 visuals cited in our current web content, 6 are in this easy-to-read category. Besides 3 photos, and an infographic, our content uses 26 area charts or pie charts.

Area charts, including stacked line graphs and pie charts, are inherently harder to read. In his book *Show Me the Numbers*, Stephen Few noted that "our visual perception is not designed to accurately assign quantitative values to 2-D areas" (Few, 2012). Few then pointed out that adding a third dimension, color, a popular graphics enhancement, only makes charts more difficult to read accurately. Additionally, visuals that convey meaning solely by color are frequently difficult to read accurately, given the fact that approximately 8% of the U.S. population is color-blind.

Color Associations and Perceptual Speed

Most people are visual learners; that is, 90 percent of what we learn comes through sight. And most of our reaction to visual stimuli (62 percent to 90 percent) is based on color (Singh, 2006). Thus, color is vital to any graphics display.

Stanford professors Lin and Heer pointed out the advantage of pairing colors with the concepts that evoke them—what they call semantically resonant color choices (Lin and Heer, 2014). At the risk of overgeneralizing, semantic resonance means you use blue for blueberries, orange for oranges, and yellow hues for bananas and lemons when charting produce items in a grocery department.

In their study published in *Harvard Business Review*, Lin and Heer asked people to complete identical comparison tasks, one using semantically resonant colors and the other using non-resonant colors. Each comparison involving semantically resonant colors took 10% less time to complete than the non-resonant comparison. Although the actual amount of time was small (one second), "these seconds add up, especially for data analysts who make untold numbers of comparisons during their workday."

Likewise, semantically resonant colors give readers the advantage of familiar color relationships, reducing their need to look at the legend accompanying the graph or chart.

Not only tangible objects but also many concepts have colors associated with them. And these associations vary from one culture to another. For example, in the U.S. culture, red is associated with danger, debt, and stop. In China, red is the color of luck. Black represents mourning in the United States; in China, white does.

The list of color meanings (Yau, 2011) in Table 1 is not comprehensive. Also, the meanings are traditional but may not be current in these cultures because old associations fade with time and multicultural awareness. The Internet, by allowing people to learn about other cultures and adopt what they like from them, has contributed greatly to the cross-cultural adoption of colors and ideas.

In his book *Visualize This*, Nathan Yau noted that though people have been graphing data for centuries, researchers began studying the relative effectiveness of various graphs only a few

Figure 2.18 (Continued)

Aadi Newar   3   April 13, 2019

Table 1 Meanings of Various Colors

Color	Western cultures	Eastern cultures
Blue	Trust, authority, conservative, corporate, peace, calm, masculinity	Immortality, femininity
Green	Luck (four-leaf clovers), spring, new birth, regeneration, nature, environmental awareness	New life, regeneration, hope, fertility
Orange	Affordable or inexpensive	Happiness, spirituality
Purple	Royalty, spirituality, wealth, fame	Wealth, sorrow, comforting, death
Yellow	Happiness, joy, hope, cowardice, caution, warning of hazards and hazardous substances	Sacred, imperial, honor, masculinity

decades ago. "In that respect," Yau wrote, "visualization is a relatively new field" (Few, 2012). The popularity of infographics may lead some business people to abandon traditional graphics. A better choice is to use the findings of visualization studies to maximize the efficacy of every visual.

Summary & Opinion

Research has shown that bar and line graphs are more easily and more accurately apprehended than are area and pie charts. An informal survey of current web content indicates that writers at Cavort Sportwear favor area and pie charts. While color theory and color associations are strictly applied to creation of Cavort's products, evidence does not indicate their use in content creation. Seemingly, colors are selected for visuals based on the current color preferences of the person producing them.

Recommendation

Given the increasing importance of data visualization, I recommend hiring a consultant to study these topics in depth. In addition, a thorough analysis of Cavort's use of various visuals seems appropriate. Then, in addition to a written report to keep for reference, an oral presentation of the consultant's results seems most fitting. Perhaps, the consultant could be retained to stay on top of trends in visual production and give us an update presentation every 12 to 18 months.

Figure 2.18 (Continued)

Aadi Newar   4   April 13, 2019

References

Few, S. (2012). *Show me the numbers: Designing tables and graphs to enlighten.* Burlingame, CA: Analytics Press.

Heer, J. (2015). The future of data visualization. You Tube. Retrieved from www.youtube.com/watch?v=vc1bq0qIKoA/

Lin, S. & Heer, J. (2014, March-April). The right colors make data easier to read. *Harvard Business Review.* Retrieved from hbr.org/2014/04/the-right-colors-make-data-easier-to-read/

Singh, S. (2006). Impact of color on marketing. *Management Decision, 44*(6), pp. 783–789. doi: 10.1108/00251740610673332

Valiela, I. (2001). *Doing science: Design, analysis, and communication of scientific research.* New York City: Oxford University Press.

Yau, N. (2011). *Visualize this: The flowing data guide to design, visualization, and statistics.* Indianapolis, IN: Wiley Publishing, Inc.

Figure 2.18 (Concluded)

Executive Summary

An executive summary is a condensed version of a longer business document, such as a business plan, research proposal, or lengthy analytical report. Typically, an executive summary identifies the analyzed issue or researched problem, reports major findings about the matter, draws concise conclusions, and recommends appropriate action. See Figure 2.19.

Some executives may read the executive summary to determine if they need to read or skim the entire report. Others read it and begin immediate action on the recommendations, without reading the full report.

An executive summary has these qualities.[44]

- Usually involves direct structure, beginning with an indication of the main conclusion(s) reached following analysis or research. The readers likely have some knowledge about the general problem and are eager to know what you, the report writer, recommend.
- Is a self-contained, stand-alone mini-report that highlights findings, conclusions, and recommendations.
- Includes only material present in the main report, but rarely repeats it verbatim.
- Omits all data displays (graphs, tables, and so on) in the report.

Executive Summary

The findings suggest that Charlestonians recognize the cruise business as an ongoing presence in the Port of Charleston and their lives. However, they want the negative aspects of that presence to be ameliorated.

To increase citizens' support for the proposed cruise terminal relocation and waterfront enhancements, the South Carolina Ports Authority must launch an extensive communication campaign. The campaign should publicize specific aspects of the concept plan, emphasizing the benefits to Charlestonians, such as improved vehicular traffic flows and parking, improved visual and human access to the waterfront, ecological reclamation and protection of the waterfront, and reclamation and protection of historical structures in the harbor. As the work progresses, the Authority should issue regular press releases to mark the progress of the project and to inform residents and merchants about construction activities that may temporarily inconvenience them. Constant communication should reassure the citizens of Charleston that the project is moving forward as planned and will soon show major benefits to residents and merchants as well as cruise passengers.

Further, as the Ports Authority proceeds with port relocation, it would be wise to simultaneously begin the proposed waterfront improvements. Such a dual approach will most readily help downtown residents and merchants experience some of the benefits of the project. The following sequence is recommended:

- Complete street construction/traffic alteration projects first.
- Upon completion of the street improvements, begin making improvements to the waterfront at the same time that construction begins on the new terminal site.

The objective of this study was to assess the business and social climate in which the South Carolina Ports Authority will operate if it implements plans to relocate the cruise terminal. Knowledge of that climate will help the Authority develop operational and communication strategies relative to the relocation. Three factors were studied:

1. What business impacts do Charleston's downtown residents and merchants perceive to be related to the arrival and departure of cruise ships?
2. What personal and community impacts do Charleston's downtown residents and merchants perceive to be related to the arrival and departure of cruise ships?
3. What knowledge of and attitudes toward relocation of the cruise terminal are evidenced by Charleston's downtown residents and merchants?

The analysis revealed that the Port Authority's plan to relocate the cruise pier and enhance the Port of Charleston incorporates many principles generally considered essential in contemporary waterfront development. Yet there is no consensus among Charleston residents and merchants about the value of the cruise industry and the proposed waterfront development.

iv

Figure 2.19 Executive summary for an analytical research report

- Contains concise paragraphs running 5% to 10% of the length of the report it accompanies. Opinions vary on appropriate length.
  - Some business people insist on confining the executive summary to a page or two. These individuals also favor the practice of using a one-page infographic (little or no text) for the executive summary.
  - Other people say a maximum of 5% of the length (report body only) is optimum. While readers need brevity, they might say, they also need enough information to choose between reading the executive summary only and reading the full report.
  - Still other business people note the increasing tendency of today's readers to read the executive summary only,

without so much as skimming the report body. To ensure adequate information for wise actions, these individuals advocate making the executive summary 10% the length of the report body. *Note*: Use the percentages as a guide to overall length of your executive summaries, but not to the length of each section. For example, an eight-page description of the study may be condensed in a sentence or two while a two-page presentation of the findings may involve a four-sentence paragraph or more.

- Demands careful revising and editing because decisions will be made based on the executive summary by people who have not read the full report.

Guides for Writing a Summation Report

The following procedure[45] will help you develop an abstract, overview, or executive summary.

1. Read the report or each journal article or blog to determine the main idea(s). As you read, ask these questions repeatedly to focus on key points.
   - What would I say if I had two minutes to talk about the subject?
   - What's the minimum information people need to know?
2. Write each main idea in a single sentence, using your own words. (To outline an executive summary, look at the titles of subsections and beginning and final sentences of paragraphs in the full report.)
3. List key facts or assertions that support the main point(s).
4. Write brief sentences containing the supporting facts or assertions.
5. Reread the report or article for background information needed to understand the main idea(s).
6. Write sentences to present the background information.
7. Combine your sentences describing the background, main idea(s), and supporting information.

8. Revise and edit your summary.
   - Eliminate unnecessary words and sentences and evaluate structure.
   - Check accuracy of spelling, grammar, and sentence and paragraph structures.
9. Produce the final summation report in an appropriate format. If you think your executive summary may be circulated separately, include the report title, your contact details, and information about obtaining the full report.

Summary

Nonroutine reports address significant problems that are job-related yet not confronted daily. The ability to prepare effective nonroutine reports—such as interview reports, feasibility reports, justification reports; press releases, fact sheets, and backgrounders; white papers; business proposals; and abstracts, overviews, and executive summaries—can have a significant effect on a person's business career.

The chapter includes reports in various formats, including business form, e-mail, infographic, and memo. In addition, it demonstrates block letter format, which is often used for external reports of one to three pages.

Before sending a business letter, check off these items, which should appear in this order.

- ☐ Sender's identification-company letterhead OR organization's typed mailing address
- ☐ Date mailed in this style: July16, 2020
- ☐ Receiver's delivery address
- ☐ Salutation, starting with Dear
- ☐ Letter body—blank space between paragraphs, no indentations
- ☐ Complimentary close—choose a standard closing like Sincerely
- ☐ Your signature lines—signed between the close and your typed name

Condensing the information obtained during an individual or group interview is the key to interview reports. When you report an individual applicant's employment interview, this checklist keeps you from omitting needed information.

☐ Candidates name and position applied for
☐ Date, time and location of interview
☐ How your information is to be used
☐ Summary of applicant's reactions to discussion topics
☐ What the interview revealed about the applicant
☐ Recap of interview results

When you report the results of a focus group interview, use this checklist to make sure the report is complete.

☐ Description of interview procedure
☐ Description of interview participants
☐ Statement of findings, or interview outcomes
☐ At least one conclusion drawn from findings
☐ At least one relevant action you recommend

Both feasibility and justification reports require the writer to recommend action and offer supporting data. A feasibility report analyzes the possible success of a significant initiative, while a justification report advocates an action and presents reasons for it. When you draft a feasibility report, use this checklist to evaluate it.

☐ Explicit recommendation to continue or discontinue the project.
☐ Complete description of the project under consideration.
☐ Data to defend your recommendation.

Justification reports differ from most other reports in two ways: They are rarely assigned but are initiated by the report writer and they involve persuading readers. This checklist may help you write persuasively.

- ☐ Try to anticipate—in detail—how the primary reader will react to your recommendation.
- ☐ As a rule, use direct structure.
- ☐ Explain the importance of your recommendation or request in terms of reader interests.
- ☐ Offset reader objections you anticipated; be open about contradictory evidence.
- ☐ Discuss resources needed to implement your recommendation.
- ☐ Summarize your report and give a CTA.
- ☐ Supply an appropriate subject line.
- ☐ When revising your draft, keep secondary readers in mind along with the primary.
- ☐ Remove any common fallacies, such as false analogy or false dilemma.

PR professionals create media kits, which always contain a press release and often include a fact sheet and backgrounder. A press release announces notable information; for example, a new executive, office, partnership, or product. When called upon to write a press release, this checklist can help you assess it.

- ☐ Name of organization
- ☐ Target date for publication
- ☐ Headline that summarizes the announcement
- ☐ Explanation of who, what, when, where, why, and how
- ☐ Contact person's name, phone number, and e-mail address

Organize the body of the press release as an inverted pyramid: answers to basic questions followed by supporting details. Use this checklist to review press release components.

- ☐ Desired release date (and hour)
- ☐ Contact information

- ☐ Bold headline
- ☐ Current date and city in which the press release originates
- ☐ The word END or ###

Use this checklist to evaluate press release content.

- ☐ Cover the 5 Ws and H in the first paragraph.
- ☐ Do not exceed 500 words.
- ☐ Insert visuals using graphic design applications like Canva and Snappa.
- ☐ Give details, not buzzwords or hype. Include a references list.
- ☐ Include quotes from significant company representatives.
- ☐ Write a headline in large, bold letters.
- ☐ Revise content; edit mechanics.
- ☐ Select the media to send to, using Muck Rack or Traacker to find appropriate ones.
- ☐ For wide-ranging circulation, use a media release distribution service like Business Wire or PR.com.
- ☐ Publish your press release on your organization's website.

For major news that can be communicated visually, use a VNR. This short checklist may help you with VNR production.

- ☐ Use lots of imagery and switch scenes often, omitting the narrator from view.
- ☐ Include interviews and plenty of cover footage.
- ☐ Make the VNR look and sound like an actual news story but identify your organization in the video.

An SMNR needs to appeal at once to traditional journalists as well as to bloggers, publishers, and the public. High-quality visual content is key. If you are involved in creating SMNR content, check off these items.

- ☐ Convey data with infographics, using apps like Easel.ly and Venngage; or hire a graphics design firm like Avalaunch and Info Graphic World.

- ☐ Use unusual fonts and calm colors.
- ☐ Insert high-resolution photos of business people at work, or post presentation slides on a site like Prezi and Speaker Deck.
- ☐ Upload 30-second videos to a hosting site, such as Cincopa and Wistia.

A fact sheet summarizes your organization and gives context to your news releases. It also may contain a range of information, such as technical data, product descriptions, and answers to FAQs.

A backgrounder includes an overview and scope of the release and company objectives, history, and basics, like location. For effective backgrounders, check off these items as you write.

- ☐ Try making journalists interested in your story.
- ☐ Give journalists more usable information than they can use.
- ☐ Use summary subheadings and graphics.
- ☐ Diligently guard against inaccuracies.
- ☐ Cite sources and include a references list for any outside research.
- ☐ Include short bios of selected company managers.
- ☐ Make backgrounders look equally good on screen and paper.
- ☐ Keep up with backgrounder writing practices at PR In Your Pajamas.

White papers can be useful for generating sales leads as they disseminate information for solving readers' business problems. As you plan a white paper, check off each item as you complete it.

- ☐ Allow several weeks to a few months, depending on difficulty of the content for the process.
- ☐ Look at sample white papers; then decide which report parts your readers will need.

☐ Choose several ways to promote your white paper, including a landing page.

☐ If it will be gated, identify precisely the information to be requested.

Readers of white papers duly expect high-quality content. They are seeking solutions for existing problems. Use this checklist to evaluate a white paper draft.

☐ Know the business problems readers face and the kinds of information current customers seek.

☐ Outline all content to save time for the writer and readers.

☐ Provide research-based content, using visuals to display data.

☐ For industry research, refer to Kompass and Wall Street ResearchTM.

☐ For government research, refer to the U.S. Government Publishing Office and Small Business Administration.

☐ For primary research, hire a research consulting firm like Forrester and Gartner.

☐ Write concisely, but thoroughly. Give readers 6 to 18 pages of substance.

☐ Give it a title that tells readers what they are getting.

☐ Revise and edit successive drafts, starting with content revision. Then edit (see Appendix A).

White paper design entails page layout, images, fonts, and colors. These elements can be used to enhance content. Use this checklist to ensure that design enriches content and helps readers.

☐ Consider posting each white paper in a sans serif font for reading on screen and a serif font for reading from paper.

☐ Use these font sizes: 14 and up, headings; 12, paragraphs; and 10, notes.

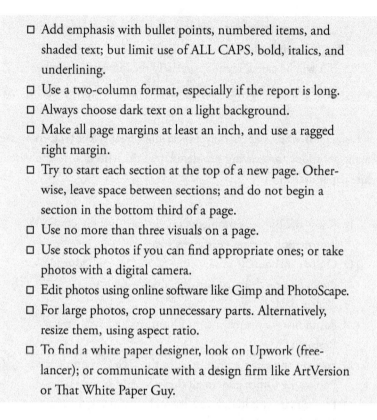

- ☐ Add emphasis with bullet points, numbered items, and shaded text; but limit use of ALL CAPS, bold, italics, and underlining.
- ☐ Use a two-column format, especially if the report is long.
- ☐ Always choose dark text on a light background.
- ☐ Make all page margins at least an inch, and use a ragged right margin.
- ☐ Try to start each section at the top of a new page. Otherwise, leave space between sections; and do not begin a section in the bottom third of a page.
- ☐ Use no more than three visuals on a page.
- ☐ Use stock photos if you can find appropriate ones; or take photos with a digital camera.
- ☐ Edit photos using online software like Gimp and PhotoScape.
- ☐ For large photos, crop unnecessary parts. Alternatively, resize them, using aspect ratio.
- ☐ To find a white paper designer, look on Upwork (freelancer); or communicate with a design firm like ArtVersion or That White Paper Guy.

Proposal writers outline a course of action and try to convince another business person to follow that course. All service, operational, and research proposals share this goal, whether solicited or unsolicited. When responding to an RFP for a product or service proposal, include the information on this checklist.

- ☐ Description of reader's need
- ☐ Description of your service
- ☐ Cost of your service
- ☐ Date for completing
- ☐ Qualifications of service provider

Whenever initiating an unsolicited operational (organizational) proposal, focus on justifying the proposed changes. This proposal is comparable to a justification report. The checklist contains just three items.

- ☐ Clear statement of proposed action
- ☐ Candid defense of the action
- ☐ Solid recap of desired action

Research proposals are usually more complex than service or operational proposals. When replying to an RFP for a research proposal, write persuasively to show that you understand the problem and that you can conduct the study. Use the following checklist to plan the research and again when drafting your proposal, though some items may be irrelevant.

- ☐ Gets or reviews your authorization.
- ☐ Identifies audience (who will get research report).
- ☐ Defines the research problem.
- ☐ States the purpose (what the study will accomplish).
- ☐ Narrows the scope (which parts of problem to study).
- ☐ States delimitations and limitations.
- ☐ Describes data collection.
- ☐ Describes the data analysis procedure.
- ☐ Estimates time schedule.
- ☐ Estimates all resources needed.
- ☐ Describes how you will present results.
- ☐ Asks approval to proceed.

Electronic signatures provide a way for turning proposals into signed contracts. Take the steps in this checklist to include an e-signature on a proposal or an accompanying contract.

- ☐ Investigate the features, pricing, and long-term validation of several online signing services like DocuSign and EverSign and choose the best one for your situation.
- ☐ Upload your proposal or contract file to the online service.
- ☐ Tag wherever you want signatures to appear.
- ☐ Enter the recipient's e-mail address and send the file.
- ☐ Whenever you receive the signed file, store it with similar files and back it up.

Your nonroutine reports may include summaries: abstracts, overviews, and executive summaries. Whenever writing any kind of summary, use this checklist as a guide.

- ☐ Read the original text; identify the main idea(s).
- ☐ In your own words, write each idea in one sentence.
- ☐ List facts and statements that support each idea; then write brief sentences using those facts.
- ☐ Reread the original text for essential background information and write sentences presenting that information.
- ☐ Blend all sentences into a cohesive summary.
- ☐ Revise first; then edit your report.
- ☐ Prepare the final report in an appropriate format.

After writing an abstract (summary of a publication), evaluate it using this checklist.

- ☐ Follows the order of the original.
- ☐ Introduces new information in each sentence.
- ☐ Contains a sentence (minimum) about each section.
- ☐ Omits minor points.
- ☐ Involves impersonal, or third-person, language.
- ☐ Omits your interpretations and opinions of the material.
- ☐ Shows the publication title in the subject line or report title.
- ☐ If over a page, includes summary subheadings.
- ☐ Highlights the author's conclusions and recommendations.
- ☐ Includes in-text citations and references in a consistent style when the author is quoted.

After preparing a topic overview, assess your report using this checklist.

- ☐ Covers who, what, when, and where with minor attention to why and how.
- ☐ Includes headings and subheadings.
- ☐ Contains a variety of visuals.

☐ Includes a glossary if the subject involves technical terms and may include a keywords list.

☐ Blends information from the various sources.

☐ Includes your interpretation and synthesis of information.

☐ Draws conclusions and recommends actions if appropriate.

Evaluate your executive summaries using this checklist.

☐ Opens with the main conclusion(s), unless you have a compelling reasons why direct structure would be inappropriate.

☐ Includes no material not found in the main report.

☐ Avoids word-for-word repetition of the report body.

☐ Omits all data displays (graphs, tables, and so on).

☐ Runs 5% to 10% the number of pages in the report it summarizes.

☐ Is carefully revised and edited.

While the variations in the reports described and illustrated here are important, remember that the success of any report depends mostly on the writer's understanding of what readers need from it.

CHAPTER 3

Writing Policies, Procedures, and Instructions

A common business reporting task involves writing policies, procedures, and instructions. These tasks may be as simple as an e-mail telling employees how to apply for a parking permit or a memo informing them of a new policy about staggered lunch breaks. In contrast, the writing projects may be as complex as preparing a brochure listing the steps for selecting benefits from the company's intranet or a complete employee manual presenting all guidelines for employment with your organization.

Employees, managers, and clients of your company will base significant decisions and actions on reports (instructions, procedures, and policies) that you write. Although the discussion and examples given in this chapter focus on policies, procedures, and instructions written for employees, the principles discussed also apply to such reports written for customers and clients.

Importance of Written Policies, Processes, and Instructions

Well-written policies, procedures, and instructions contribute to organizational efficiency and effectiveness, although these reports have common characteristics, they differ in why they are written and how they are used.

Significance of Policies

Policies define an organization's view on specific issues or problems and indicate how the organization will handle problems when they arise. Specifically, policies have these effects.

- Explain desired behavior of individuals associated with the organization, helping to define its culture.
- Create a foundation for making sound, timely decisions throughout the organization, not just in the human resources area.
- Describe the nature of the employer–employee relationship, including its benefits and obligations, both mundane—such as parking policies—and substantive—such as accepting gifts from suppliers or giving gifts to potential clients.
- Policies impact employees' lives. So, all policies should be set fairly, communicated clearly, and applied consistently. The best way to do so: Put the policies in writing and ensure that all employees have access to them, whether in print or online. (A well-written employee manual—discussed later in this chapter—serves that purpose.)

A policy concerning employee use of the employer's information technology (IT) appears in Figure 3.1.

One employment policy expert identified 10 policies as vital to all but the very smallest organizations.[1]

- *Customer quality policy*. Defines what clients or customers want from your organization's products or services.
- *Customer credit policy*. Explains credit and payment terms, how to open new accounts, and the criteria for collecting amounts due.
- *Ethics policy*. Outlines your organization's stance on customers' privacy and information security, how you avoid conflicts of interest, and other ethical, or fair treatment, subjects.
- *Employment policies*. Explains the designated work hours, the at-will relationship between employer and employees, how performance reviews are conducted, and rules for employment termination.
- *Harassment and discrimination policies*. Specifies the conditions of equal opportunity employment (EEO)—no age, sex, race, or cultural bias. Includes clear guidelines on how the

7. Information Technology (IT) Policy

7.1 General Policy

The company's computer, phone, and voicemail systems are intended for the sole purpose of supporting the company's business needs. Use of those systems is a privilege, not a right. All employees are expected to use those systems only for business-related purposes.

7.2 Confidentiality of Information

Business-related information contained in the electronic systems, including email, is considered confidential and should be disclosed to authorized employees only.

No employee has a personal privacy right in any matter created, received, or sent through electronic or voicemail or in files and data residing on her or his assigned computer, external storage device, computer system, or voicemail.

7.3 Software Ownership and Use

Only organization-authorized software is permitted on the organization's computers. Installation of non-company (third party) computer programs is allowed only with the express permission of the information systems manager.

All software, files, and/or data loaded into the organization's computer network become the property of the organization. Such files or software may be used only in ways consistent with their licenses or copyrights.

No games of any type are permitted.

System users are not to abuse Internet access privileges.

- o   The company's system is not to be used to violate the law by downloading or distributing pirated information.

- o   The company's system is not to be used to download or transmit material that is offensive, obscene, vulgar, or threatening.

7.4 Monitoring of Use

The company will monitor the IT system to ensure that it is being used for business purposes. The company may inspect computer files on any of its computers or terminals without notice and at any time.

Responsibility and authority to inspect computer files, computer terminals, email, and voicemail is vested in the president and CEO or her/his designate.

7.5 Violation

Improper use of the company's IT system may be grounds for discipline, including immediate discharge.

Figure 3.1 Typical business employee policy

organization handles employee diversity, including, but not limited to, handicap and pregnancy.

- *Compensation and benefits policies.* Describes the company's position on holidays, vacation, and sick leave; the medical insurance coverage, other benefits, and retirement plans offered; and how payroll, salary and wage increases, and bonuses are handled.
- *IT policies and procedures.* Outlines acceptable Internet and social media use during work hours, the availability of third-party software for employee's use, and the organization's stand on malware and technical support (as shown in Figure 3.1).
- *Discipline policy.* Explains how the organization will respond to employee misconduct, including theft, poor performance,

and substance abuse at work. Also describes the appeal and
reinstatement policy for a terminated employee.

- *Purchasing policy.* Clarifies who (by job title) is authorized
  to make purchases and sign checks for the organization,
  how competitive bids are handled, and other standards for
  how employees spend company money.
- *Workplace safety policy and procedures.* Describes required
  safety equipment and clothing and prohibit unsafe attitudes
  and activities.

Importance of Procedures

A procedure tells how a series of sequential tasks should be performed
to achieve a specific outcome.[2] Procedures often accompany a policy,
explaining how to implement it. Procedures may describe who does what
and when, while others may be less specific. A procedure accompanies the
reimbursement policy in Figure 3.2 (see three parts of Section 9.4).

To distinguish procedures from instructions, one writer defined a procedure this way: ten separate actions, three or more small tasks, steps and
sub-steps, and completed from start to finish in one sitting (no major
delays between steps).[3] The straightforward bookkeeping procedure in
Figure 3.3 fits this definition. Notice that the procedure indicates tasks to
be completed and includes some how-to information.

A procedure may be conveyed in a flowchart rather than in text. Some
flowcharts use a rectangle or a square for each element, but many flowchart designers use the standard symbols shown in Figure 3.4.

A flowchart describing the procedure for making electronic payments
is shown in Figure 3.5 (p. 157).

Sometimes multiple procedures are combined to describe three or
more medium to large tasks, to be completed by more than one person
or department, with hours, days, or weeks between steps. These combined procedures represent a process. In writing, a process is less detailed
than a procedure.[4] Figure 3.6 (p. 158) shows one of 27 procedures in a
construction safety process, described in a 96-page manual. Notice that
this page states what tasks are to be done but does not specify how to
accomplish them.

---

9. Reimbursement of Relocation Expenses

9.1 Purpose

The company will reimburse a new employee for relocation expenses when such reimbursements are considered essential to successful recruitment of the job candidate. Partial or full reimbursement may be allowed.

9.2 Scope

Relocation expenses may be reimbursed for the moving of household goods and personal effects for the employee and the members of her or his household. The reimbursement will cover the cost of packing, crating, and transporting the goods and personal effects from the former home to the new home. Travel and lodging expenses incurred during travel from the former home to the new home may also be covered.

Non-reimbursable expenses are meals while moving from the old residence to the new residence; meals, travel, and lodging expenses for pre-move, house-hunting trips; and stays in temporary quarters while getting settled into the new residence.

9.3 Definitions

Relocation expenses must comply with deductible moving expenses as defined by the Internal Revenue Service, unless those expenses are specifically excluded under Sec. 9.2.

9.4 Procedure

9.4.1 Direct Expenditure Voucher

Reimbursement for relocation expenses must be processed on Form DEV, Direct Expenditure Voucher.

9.4.2 Required Documentation

A copy of the moving company invoice is required for partial or full reimbursement.

If full reimbursement for moving is allowed, two quotes must accompany the DEV and invoice. Only the lower amount will be reimbursed, even if the company with the lower quote is not used.

If partial reimbursement is allowed, the amount to be paid must be specified by the employee's supervisor, as indicated in Sec. 9.4.3.

9.4.3 Responsibilities

The employee is responsible for obtaining the two quotes from licensed movers, providing the copy of the moving company's invoice, and completing Form DEV.

After reviewing all materials, the employee's supervisor shall insert the appropriate code to indicate the account to be charged, enter the amount of reimbursement, sign the form to indicate authorization, and submit the required documentation to the Human Resources Division for review and approval.

Human Resources shall forward all approved requests to the Accounting Division for payment. Unapproved requests shall be returned to the employee's supervisor with an explanation of the reasons for non-approval.

Accounting will make reimbursement directly to the employee at the address indicated on the DEV.

Figure 3.2 Policy including an implementation procedure (Section 9.4)

Because a process involves several people, it cannot be shown clearly in a flowchart. The alternate is a process map. A process map consists of two or more rows containing standard symbols. Each row represents one department or job title. Thus, the map shows who is responsible for each action in the process. Process maps are time consuming to draw but convey complex information clearly.[5] The map in Figure 3.7 (p. 158) shows processing of orders for CDs placed with sales representatives.

Accounting Procedures   **Photos by Kelvin**

Procedure for Quarter-End Closing in QuickBooks Software

Close organization accounts at the end of each quarter. Thus, our accounting records and tax liabilities are locked down for each quarter. Using QuickBooks business accounting software, close accounts quarterly by setting each preferred closing date and a closing date password. The password prevents any unauthorized person from changing the accounts after the closing date.

1. Launch QuickBooks. In the main menu bar, select Edit. In the pull-down menu, select Preferences. The Preferences window opens.

2. From the list on the left, select Accounting and click the "Company Preferences" tab.

3. In the Company Preferences pane, scroll to the Closing Date section and click the Set Date/Password button.

4. Select the date on which you want to close the organization's accounts (MAR 31, JUN 30, SEP 30, or DEC 31).

5. Select "Exclude estimates, sales orders, and purchase orders from closing date restrictions." Thus, you exclude non-posting financial transactions from the closing.

6. Type your assigned password in the Closing Date Password field; retype it in the Confirm Password field. Thus, you restrict access to the closed accounts. *Note:* In two or three secure places, record this password and closing date. If your password is changed for any reason, the closed accounts can be accessed using the password you recorded.

7. To complete the procedure, click OK.

Figure 3.3 A procedure for completing bookkeeping tasks

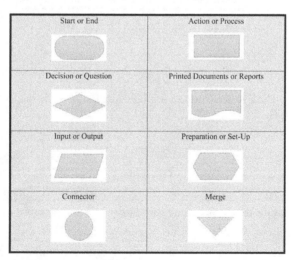

Figure 3.4 Flowchart symbols

Source: SmartDraw. (n.d.). "Flowchart Symbols."

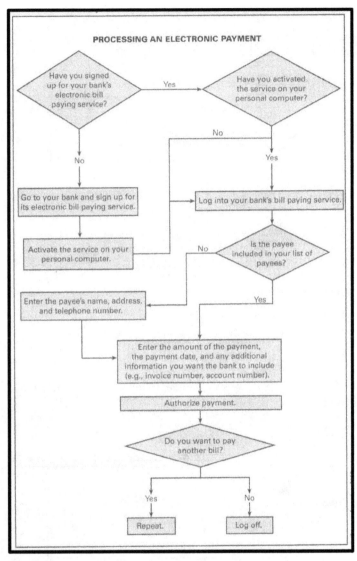

Figure 3.5 Flowchart representing a procedure

Source: Kuiper and Clippinger.

Importance of Work Instructions

Instructions provide detailed directions for completing a task. Instructions generally describe tasks having fewer than 10 separate actions performed by one person during a short timeframe.[6] Explaining to an employee how

The URI Organization   *Construction Project Safety Procedures Manual*

11. HOUSEKEEPING

This procedure is designed to outline the project housekeeping requirements for all contractors to maintain a clean and safe work environment.

A. Introduction

All contractors are required to maintain their respective work areas in clean, orderly, and sanitary condition always.

B. Maintenance

- Each contractor is responsible for arranging for the removal of all scrap material generated during each project.
- During alteration, construction, renovation, or repairs, keep all construction debris clear from all work areas and do not allow debris to accumulate.
- Properly dispose of all materials according to federal, state, and local guidelines.
- Contractors shall ensure that enough trash receptacles are located within their respective work areas.
- On containers to be discarded, clearly mark the contents; for example, METAL, OILY RAGS, PAPER WASTE.
- Provide covers for containers used to collect garbage, solvents, other flammable wastes, and hazardous wastes, such as acids and caustics.
- Arrange building materials so that they do not pose a hazard to personnel in or around the area.
- Maintain walking and working surfaces clear of materials and or debris. Cords and hoses must be out of walkways or elevated 7 feet above floor level.
- Glass containers are not allowed on site.

Under no circumstances is the Contractor to leave the jobsite for the day until each of the above Maintenance requirements is fulfilled. The Contractor shall provide periodic cleanup during the day as necessary to provide working conditions that are clean, orderly, safe, and sanitary.

C. Sanitation

- Contractors shall ensure that there is an adequate supply of drinking water for their employees.
- Contractors shall provide single-use cups.
- Water containers must be tightly closed and equipped with a tap.
- The water dispenser shall have tape on the lid showing the date and time the water was prepared.
- Provide a trash receptacle near each water dispenser.
- Water containers must be cleaned daily.
- Contractors must provide sufficient toilet facilities onsite for their personnel.

41

Figure 3.6 Housekeeping is just one of many procedures in the construction safety process

Source: Office of Capital Projects.

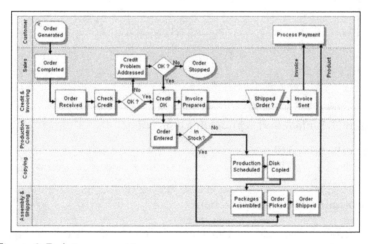

Figure 3.7 A process map

Source: Business Process Mapping.

to use the company's intranet to select employee benefits requires step-by-step instructions. Often, instructions are written for people trained to do the task but who need to review the steps to improve performance.

Most instructions emphasize correct and safe performance of a task. Thus, instructions protect employees and the employer. For example, Clear, accurate instructions for removing worn tires and installing new tires on a customer's automobile—if followed—help a technician perform the task in the most efficient manner and protect her or him from injury. Those properly followed instructions can also protect the employer by reducing employee compensation claims for on-the-job injuries and avoiding liability suits by car owners should accidents occur.

The typical work instructions shown in Figures 3.8a to 3.8j explain how to operate an organization's upscale printer-copier-fax machine-scanner. (Online User's Guide available at http://solutions.brother.com/manuals).

Figure 3.8a Work instructions show the meaning of icons and font styles used throughout

Source: Basic User's Guide.

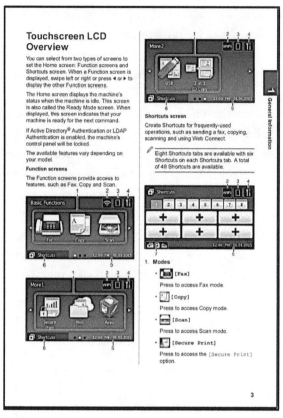

Figure 3.8b Instructions with labeled visuals

Note: Observe the Tips icon, explained in Figure 3.8a.

Although policies, procedures, and instructions differ in content and purpose, certain general writing guides apply to all of them.

Basic Guides for Writing
Policies, Procedures, and Instructions

Policies, procedures, and instructions can be difficult to write because language is easily misinterpreted. For that reason, these reports are often drafted, reviewed by experts, and revised many times before they are released.

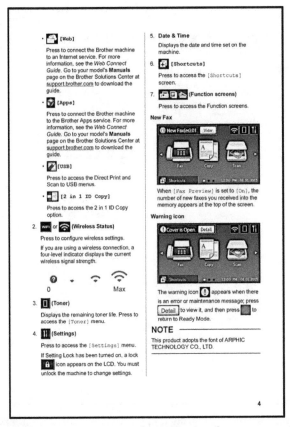

Figure 3.8c Instructions page with ample visuals, a note, and a warning icon

The following basic guides for writing these items are much like those for all business reports.

- *Analyze your audience.* Identify specifically who will read your report.
  - o Identifying employees as the audience may be insufficient. Example: Your company adds a 40l(k) plan to its benefits roster. The policy regarding participation and amount that may be dedicated to the plan must be written so that all employees—from executives with MBA degrees to shop workers who have not completed high school—can understand why and how to participate in the plan.

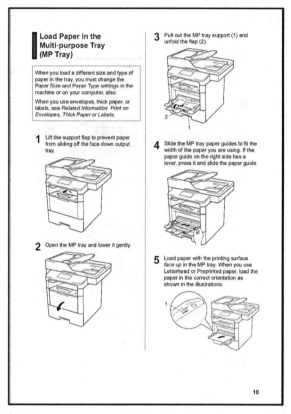

Figure 3.8d Instructions using a clear heading, large numbers for the steps, and arrows that clarify the task

Note: For showing detail, line drawings are more effective than photos.

- o Then ask yourself the following questions.
  - How will the audience perceive what I write?
  - What is the audience's likely attitude toward the policy, procedure, or instructions?
  - Will the audience perceive the policy as a genuine benefit to employees or as an attempt by management to manipulate or control them?
    Example: A major employer offered the IRS-approved medical spending account to its employees. Thus, employees could request the employer to withhold

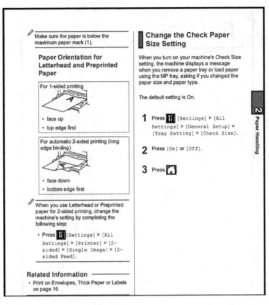

Figure 3.8e Work instructions providing tips, related information, and section name and number

Note: Blank space gives the user a rest and allows the next instruction to start at the top of the page.

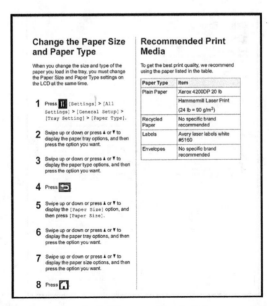

Figure 3.8f Instructions including a table that presents information clearly and concisely

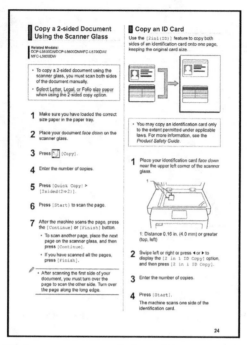

Figure 3.8g Task instructions including all steps, even those that may seem obvious and unnecessary

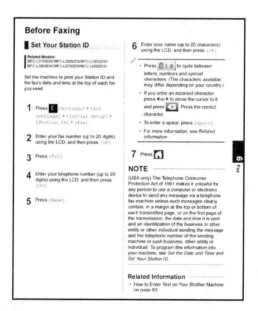

Figure 3.8h Notes and tips providing important information that is clearly set apart from the action steps

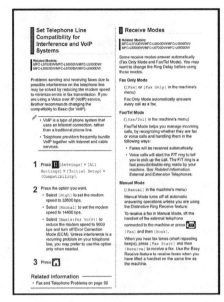

Figure 3.8i *Easy reading assured through use of blank space, lines, columns, bullets, bold, and bars*

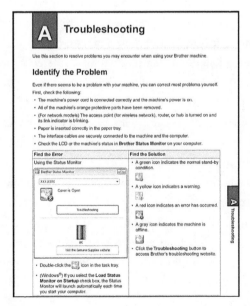

Figure 3.8j *Work instructions showing what to do when something goes wrong*

Source: Basic User's Guide.

pretax dollars to set aside for out-of-pocket medical expenses. Employees had full discretion to specify the amount to be withheld (up to federal limits) and submitted receipts for reimbursement. Thus, employees could pay for certain medical expenses with tax-free money.

However, some employees resisted the program, declaring that it was a way for the business manager to "hang onto our money a little longer." The person who wrote the policy and the procedures for participating described the plan clearly but did not consider the climate of suspicion that prevailed in the organization at the time.

- *Identify the context.* Determine when, where, and how your employees will use the report.
  - o Is the report intended as a reference tool to be consulted only when a specific question arises?
  - o Do you want the user to read the report carefully before acting, or do you expect the person to read the report while performing a step-by-step procedure?
  - o How will cultural and international differences affect the interpretation of a policy or the understanding of the language used to define steps in instructions?
- *Define your goal.* Ask yourself what you want the reader to do or be able to do after reading the report. Then link your goal to your analysis of audience and context: Who must be able to do what, in what way, to what extent, and under what circumstances?

  Example: When writing policies and procedures to apply for a reserved parking space, you should identify:
  - o all types of employees who are affected by the policy
  - o when they are most likely to read the policy and procedures
  - o everything you want them to do in the procedure

o whether it is important for employees to complete all
    steps of the procedure

If your company provides preferred parking for
employees who carpool, those who do so would have to
complete certain parts of the application procedure that
others would not be required to complete. The policy must
clearly identify the criteria to qualify for preferred parking,
and the procedure must indicate clearly which steps must
be completed by employees who want to be considered for
preferred parking.

- *Write to achieve clarity, consistency, completeness, and gender
  equity.* As you write your report, always ask what you can
  do to make the information easy to use and understand.
  o *To achieve clarity:*
     - Use simple declarative sentences with active verbs and
       limited modifiers.
     - Avoid legalese or overly formal language like that in
       the following example.
       Example: All full-time employees are hereby noti-
       fied that they should not pursue employment that
       may unduly interfere with their timely arrival at the
       Company and pursuit of Company expectations.
     - Avoid ambiguous terms, such as reasonable or
       excessive.
     - Use concrete language—words that are likely to have
       the same meaning for all readers.
     - In addition, explain any acronyms (abbreviations
       formed from the initial letters of other words and
       pronounced as a word,[7] such as DoD, GAAP, HIPAA,
       and IEEE. *Note*: Department of Defense, Generally
       Accepted Accounting Principles, Health Insurance
       Portability and Accountability Act of 1996, and
       Institute of Electrical and Electronics Engineers,
       respectively.

Figures 3.1 and 3.2 demonstrate unambiguous policies. As you review these figures, notice that the text clearly accomplishes several things:

- Gives the rationale for the policy
- Identifies to whom the policy applies
- Identifies standards that are to be met
- Lists consequences of violating the policy

o *To achieve consistency*, use the same words to describe the same thing. For example, wage rates can be described as base rate, hourly rate, straight-time rate, or other descriptors. However, when writing policies and so on, you should choose one term and use it consistently throughout a policy. Figure 3.9, a combination policy (Sections 11.1 to 11.3) and procedure (Sections 11.4 to 11.6), repeats the words discrimination and harassment. In no instance is either word replaced with a synonym.

o *To achieve completeness*, whenever a policy or procedure is modified, review all related policies and procedures to ensure that they are complete and consistent with the modifications. A change in one policy could well require a review of the entire set.

Example: The policy-procedure in Figure 3.2 refers to Form DEV (Direct Expense Voucher). If that form were to be renamed and assigned a form number, this policy-procedure—and any others that refer to the form—must be changed accordingly.

o *To achieve gender equity*, avoid the long-outdated practice of referring to employees as he or him.

- When it is logical to do so, use plural nouns and pronouns (employees ... they).
- If the sentence logically requires a singular noun (employee, associate), refer to the noun with two singular pronouns, such as her or his, he or she. (See Figure 3.1, Section 7.4, and Figure 3.9, Section 11.2.)
- A third option involves repeating nouns rather than referring to them with pronouns.

11. Discrimination or Harassment

11.1 General Policy

The company endeavors to maintain a work environment that nourishes respect for the dignity of each individual. Acts of discrimination by supervisors or co-workers, including sexual or racial harassment, are strictly prohibited and may result in disciplinary action, depending on the circumstances, up to and including termination.

11.2 Supervisor and Employee Conduct

Unwelcome racial or sexual conduct that interferes with an individual's job performance or creates an intimidating, hostile, or offensive environment is strictly prohibited. All employees, including both supervisory and nonsupervisory personnel, are prohibited from engaging in unwelcome sexual conduct or making unwelcome sexual overtures, either verbal or physical. Such prohibited conduct includes, but is not limited to, offensive and unwelcome sexual flirtations, advances, or propositions; repeated verbal abuse of a sexual or racial nature; graphic or degrading comments about an individual or his or her appearance; the display of sexually suggestive objects or pictures; or any offensive or abusive physical contact. NOTE: Women are not the only persons who experience sexual harassment; men also experience sexual harassment, and harassment can occur between persons of the same sex.

11.3 Supervisor Conduct

Each supervisor is responsible for maintaining a discrimination-free environment. Supervisors are strictly prohibited from implying or stating that submitting or refusing to submit to sexual advances will have any effect on an individual's hiring, placement, compensation, training, promotion, or any other term or condition of employment.

11.4 Procedure for Employees

When possible, the person experiencing discrimination or harassment should clearly explain to the offending party that the behavior is causing discomfort. Ask that it cease immediately. If it continues, employees should immediately report any incident that they believe to be discrimination or harassment to their supervisor or the Director of Human Resources.

11.5 Investigation

Complaints of discrimination or harassment will be promptly investigated by the complaining employee's supervisor and/or the Director of Human Resources. The investigation should be conducted as impartially and confidentially as possible. At the end of the investigation, the supervisor and/or Director of Human Resources should advise the complaining employee of the results of the investigation and the disciplinary action to be taken, if any.

11.6 Discipline

Any employee who is found to have engaged in harassment of another employee will be subject to disciplinary action, up to and including termination.

Figure 3.9 Policy-procedure demonstrating consistency

Content Guides and Best Practices: Policies, Procedures, and Instructions

Before you can plan (analyze audience, identify context, and define goal) or draft (aim for clarity, consistency, completeness, and gender equity), of course, you must be conversant with the content. The following lists provide that information.

Policy Content

A policy, as already noted, states a position and is the least detailed of the three.

The following list recommends the content and organization of policies.[8]

- *Title.* Give the policy a name that employees will immediately recognize.
- *Introduction.* Give the purpose of the policy and state to whom it applies. (The first sentence under General Policy in Figures 3.1, 3.2, and 3.9 presents the purpose.) Also, define any terms that may be unfamiliar to the employees.
- *Body.* Describe conditions addressed by the procedure and related policy, if any. Specify who is responsible for carrying out these conditions. If an organization is responsible, write its name in full.
- *Conclusion.* State the disciplinary actions resulting from policy violations. (A typical conclusion is brief and open-ended as shown in Figures 3.1 and 3.9.) Also, indicate any other documents the policy refers to and how to access them.

Procedure Content

A procedure tells how a series of tasks should be done to reach a specific outcome and is more detailed than a policy.[9] Include features in the following list that apply to your situation. However, omit features included in an accompanying policy and combine features to avoid repetition or improve clarity.[10]

- *Purpose.* State the rationale for and importance of the procedure.
- *Scope.* Explain who and what activities are affected by the procedure, including where input comes from (supplies) and where output goes (customers).
- *Definitions.* Define all terms readers need to know to follow the procedure.

- *Responsibilities.* Identify who performs what actions and when.
- *Criteria.* Provide means for knowing when the outcome is as expected.
- *Standards.* Specify any quality management system (QMS) that applies, such as ISO 9001, iSixSigma, or Sarbanes-Oxley. *Note*: Coverage of QMS is beyond the scope of this book. For information, search keywords "quality management system" and see the websites of ISO,[11] iSixSigma,[12] and Sarbanes-Oxley (SOX).[13]
- *Feedback.* State whether feedback data should be recorded. Indicate what should be recorded and in what form (graphs, reports, worksheets, and tables).
- *Regulations.* Write about any federal, state, or local laws that apply.
- *Attachments.* Provide items to facilitate the procedure—for instance, sample forms and explanatory material alluded to in the procedure.
- *References.* Refer to any related documents readers may need to consult in following the procedure.

Work Instructions Content and Best Practices

An instruction explains step by step how to perform a certain task and is the most detailed. Be sure you understand all technical details before you begin writing or drawing. Ideally, you will visualize the task so you can describe each action to be taken and the exact sequence of them.[14]

Work instructions content:

- *Introduction.* Orient the reader to the task. Define it and describe where, when, and why it is performed.
    o If only individuals who have a certain skill level should perform the task, identify the level of expertise required.

- o Provide an overview of the task or the theory behind the task to help a reader understand the desired outcome and identify when an error has been made.
- o Include a description of the conditions under which the task should be performed and the time required. Imagine, for example, the frustration you would experience if, in the middle of a task, you were to discover that you do not have time to complete it.
- *Warnings and special notes.* Alert readers to the possibility of damaging the equipment, making an error, or hurting themselves.
  - o Identify warnings or safeguards very clearly (perhaps with standard icons for warning or caution) and explain the reason for the warning—what will happen if the caution is disregarded.
  - o Place warnings at the beginning of the report and again at crucial points within the instructions.
- *Technical background or theory.* For some procedure, the technical principles or background is critical. For example, instructions for making a hardware sorting tray include the following statements: "Sides of the tray are attached to the front and back using tongue and dado joinery. The bottom of the tray is rabbeted to fit in a groove. For the sorting surface, I used a piece of melamine."[15] To understand those instructions, the reader needs background in woodworking and the use of power tools.
- *Equipment and supplies.* List items to be gathered before the reader starts the task. A vertical checklist will help the reader assemble the necessary items and avoid the frustration of discovering in the process that some required materials are missing.
- *Discussion of the steps.* As you describe the steps in performing the task, number and name each step.
  - o Limit each step to one action.
  - o Order the steps into the required sequence.

- Use a vertical, numbered list for steps that must be done in a fixed order.
- Use a vertical, bulleted list for steps that may be done in any order.
- If you present alternate steps (two or more ways to do something), use a bulleted list with OR inserted between the alternatives or a lead-in line that indicates you are presenting alternatives.
- In a complex task, indent substeps more and label them a, b, c, and so on.
  o Highlight any exceptions. Use a unique symbol to flag an exception and explain how to accommodate it.
  o If you must present supplementary information for clarity, distinguish supplementary information from the instructions that make up the step. Place supplementary information in a separate paragraph or use a bold font for the instruction step.

Work instructions best practices:

- Ask yourself: Am I the most appropriate person to be writing work instructions, given my knowledge of the process and its pitfalls and safety issues?
  o If so, interview workers who complete the task daily for help.
  o If not, engage a professional business writing service, such as one of these.
    - Cherryleaf (https://www.cherryleaf.com)
    - Dan Furman's Clear Writing (www.clear-writing.com)
    - Probizwriters, LLC (www.probizwriters.com/index. php)
    - TwoDogBlog (https://twodogblog.biz)
- Also consider using work instructions software for increased efficiency as you write. Examples include these programs.

- o Assembly X (www.assemblyxsoftware.com)
- o Dozuki (www.dozuki.com/solutions/electronic-work-instructions)
- o Ease Works (https://easeinc.beaconquality.com/products/visual-work-instructions)
- o eFlex Systems (https://www.eflexsystems.com/work-instruction-software)
- o PSI—Production Software Integrated (https://www.productionsoft .com)
- o VKS—Visual Knowledge Share (https://www.vksapp.com/book-demo)

- Confirm that work instructions match information provided in worker training sessions.
- Ensure that instructions can be accessed easily and quickly. Ideally, keep instructions on display in the workplace. Arrange written instructions so users can skim-read them.
- Make instructions concise by including only essential information and using ample visuals. While we remember 10% of what we read, adding visuals increases our memory rate to 20%—and a video demonstration raises the rate to 30%.
  - o Show any objects your instructions refer to.
  - o Show before and after photos and right versus wrong situations.
  - o Take photos daily for use in written instructions.
- Use simple language: short, specific words and short sentences (roughly 15 to 25 words). Using action verbs instead of passive ones helps you keep sentences short.
- Write in the present tense, using many imperative verbs and the pronoun you, so each reader will see herself or himself as the person who performs the task.
- Review your policies as thoughtfully as you (or the technical writer you hired) wrote them. A 7Cs checklist, containing attributes mentioned previously in this chapter, will remind you what to look for: content, consistency,

> completeness, control, compliance, correctness, and clarity. Ask a worker who will use the instructions to review them, too.
>
> • If work instructions must be changed after employees use them, revise and redistribute the written or drawn or video version. If changes are conveyed orally, workers will likely stop trusting—and stop using—the written instructions.
>
> • Arrange all instructions the same way so users know where to find each type of information, such as cautions, machine settings, and required tools.
>
> • Always test instructions on the kind of person they were written for.

Employee Manuals

An employee manual provides a single source for all policies and procedures and some instructions related to the employer–employee relationship. Other names for this single source include[16]:

• Company Procedures Manual
• Corporate Training Manual
• Employee Handbook
• Employee Policy Manual
• Operations Manual
• Personnel Policy Manual
• Policy and Procedure Manual

Note: Some experts distinguish operations, policy, and training manuals; but generally, these names are used interchangeably. A management team might decide to break with tradition and attract readers by giving the manual a title with more sparkle, for example, "The Way Things Work at Masella Law."

Though many laws require employers to notify employees of certain workplace rights, no federal or state law requires an employer to have an employee manual. Consequently, many employers do not use one.

However, in companies that use one, the employee handbook is seen as a vital tool to employers and employees alike. Also, creating and maintaining an employee manual is viewed as best practice.

Advantages to Employees and Employers

For employers, manuals ensure consistency in supervisory decisions. For employees, manuals inform them of their employment rights and responsibilities within the organization. The following list cites additional advantages of an employee manual.[17]

Advantages for employees:

- Tells the organization's success story, creating enthusiasm for joining the company and pride in its corporate culture.
- Tells what is important to the organization.
- Provides quick answers to many employees' questions.
- Indicates to employees that the employer wants to be fair.
- Tells employees what is expected of them on the job and spells out their earned benefits and compensation.
- Tells what to expect from the employer in response to their complaints and problems.
- Assures employees that individuals with similar problems will be treated similarly.

Advantages for employers:

- Eliminates the need to decide most questions on a case-by-case basis and makes upper-level managers' jobs easier by announcing the same rules to all employees.
- Provides a plan for ethical and legal treatment of employees, protecting employers from lawsuits—such as harassment, wrongful termination, and discrimination claims.
- Outlines a plan for progressive employee discipline and a procedure for filing complaints, so that employees are not surprised if their actions warrant disciplinary action.

- Serves as a guide for resolution of disputes about employee treatment.
- Provides for an agreeable, impartial, and supportive work environment.

However, unless the manual is written and reviewed extremely carefully, it may confuse and frustrate employees and weaken the employer's case in disputes. Therefore, when you are responsible for contributing to an employee manual, be aware of legal considerations and apply writing standards that will not compromise the organization's position but will, instead, enable readers to be well-informed, confident employees.

Manual Content Guides

An employee manual should contain these three types of policies:

- Requirements of employment (regulations, rules, standards, and so on)
- Benefits of employment (holidays, insurance, vacations, and so forth)
- Policies to satisfy legal requirements or to protect the organization against legal action (overtime pay, sexual harassment, family and medical leave provisions, and the like)

Well-accepted content recommendations for employee manuals include specific topics in these three categories along with a few additional topics.[18]

Requirements of employment:

- *Procedures for completing required forms*, including income tax withholding, proof of identity and eligibility for employment according to the U.S. Immigration Reform and Control Act of 1986, proof of a completed drug test by a designated medical center, and others.

- *Attendance policy.* Give specific rules and standards. Include how many hours in advance employees must notify their supervisors if they are going to be absent or late. Also define job abandonment (voluntary resignation).
- *Description of how employees are to behave and communicate* in the workplace. Include a contact person that employees can speak to if necessary.
- *Rules concerning employees' personal use of the organization's systems*—computer hardware and software, e-mail, instant messaging, Internet, mail, motor vehicles, mobile devices, social media, and SMS (texting)—both at work and off-site. Include rules about employees' use of personal mobile devices during the workday.
- *Expectations for employees keeping certain business information confidential,* including inspection, release, or retrieval of employee records.
- *Standards for employees' attire and grooming at work,* including the dress code, if any, with visual examples. Include beards, head apparel (which may have cultural or religious significance), visible tattoos, and the like, as well as any required safety attire.

Benefits of employment:

- *Definitions of full- and part-time employment, work week, and overtime.* Include benefits of full- and part-timers, along with timekeeping procedures; flexible work schedules (flextime), if any; and information about meal and rest breaks.
- *Description of employee benefits,* such as dental and medical plans, life insurance, and retirement and savings plans. Explain who is eligible, criteria for enrolling, and when an employee can change benefits. Avoid too much detail, which may change often.

Satisfying legal requirements:

- *Declaration of equal employment opportunity and non-discrimination.* State that the organization prohibits all types of discrimination in the workplace, including compliance with Americans with Disabilities Act (ADA).
- *Information about different types of leave* (holidays, paid time off, sick leave, and bereavement, military, personal, and voting leave). Include provisions of the U.S. Family and Medical Leave Act of 1993, if applicable. *Note*: Employers are required by federal law to have leave policies in place.
- *Policies for employee conduct*, including unexplained absence, alcohol and drug use, sexual harassment, theft, and violence; plus, grounds for suspension (laid off) and termination and due process. Include procedure for filing grievances and communicating work-related issues with supervisors and managers.
- *Policies for demotion, promotion, and transfer.* Also, explain how and when employee performance reviews are conducted.
- *Procedures for handling accidents at work* that result in injury.
- *Disclaimer that the employee manual is NOT a contract* between employer and employee. Additionally, include a companion statement that an employee can be dismissed at the organization's discretion.

Additional topics:

- *Welcome message with a brief description of the organization's history,* reasons for success, and how current employees can contribute to future success.
- *Outline of the manual's importance and purpose.*

- *Organization's mission or purpose with historical information and goals.*
- *Rules and procedures for travel* and reimbursement of expenses.
- *Procedures for terminating employment through resignation or retirement;* also, exit interviews.

The preceding contents list includes standard policies included in virtually all employee manuals. For a comprehensive list of potential topics, see Heathfield's article on that subject.[19]

Legal Considerations

Employment rules differ among jurisdictions. In general, though, U.S. employment law assumes an at-will relationship; that is, either party may terminate employment at any time without cause, and the employer may change the terms of employment without notice. In some states, statements in employee manuals have been held to modify the at-will assumption, regardless of the employer's intentions. Other states have held that employee manuals are general guides that do not alter the at-will status. Therefore, before producing a manual for employees in the United States, determine your state's requirements.[20]

On the subject of at-will employment, the American Bar Association advised employers as follows.[21]

- Avoid terms such as just cause or proper cause when describing discipline or termination policies and procedures. These terms tend to erode the at-will concept, because an employee may claim the cause was not just or that he or she was not granted progressive discipline.
- Also avoid reference to probationary, orientation, or training periods. Such terms may suggest that after the period has lapsed, the employee is protected beyond the at-will status.

- Instruct supervisors not to make statements that suggest guarantees of employment or benefits.
- Additionally, consider union contract conflict. Clarify the degree to which the employee manual does or does not apply to employees who are covered by a union contract. Such clarification can be provided in the introduction, at the beginning of specific manual sections, or both.

Obtain Signed Acknowledgments of Receipt

A common practice involves putting an acknowledgment of receipt form into the employee manual for each employee to sign and return. In at-will states, this form naturally emphasizes the at-will employment provision. In Figure 3.10, bullets call attention to the at-will information.

The form illustrated in Figure 3.10 asks employees to sign off on receiving the manual, but not on reading all of it. Traditionally, this acknowledgment form would have included a statement like this: "I have read and understand the contents of this manual and will act in accordance with these policies and procedures as a condition of my employment at Masella Law." As you might assume, such a statement led employees to be less than honest. The natural tendency is to refer to the employee manual as needed. Expecting new employees to read and comprehend the manual from beginning to end on their own time is simply not practical. Employers who truly want employees to read the handbook must allocate work time for them to do so.[23] Perhaps a better way to help employees understand the manual is to present highlights of a selected policy at each team meeting.[24]

Seek Legal Counsel

Though you may follow all the foregoing guides while writing employment policies and developing the employee manual, you want to leave nothing to chance. Always have your manual reviewed by legal counsel! *Note*: If you purchase a template (editable Word files that you download and customize for your organization) from, say, Bizmanualz,[25] ConvergePoint,[26]

Figure 3.10 Form for employees to acknowledge receiving the manual

Source: Adapted from Heathfield article at thebalancecareers.com[22]

or SampleTemplates[27] do not make an exception. A review by specialists in employment law helps to further ensure that the manual will serve the employer's and employees' best interests.

Do Frequent Updates

Likewise, the employee manual should be reviewed and revised periodically to reflect changes in the organization, laws, society, and technology. In a dynamic business environment, a manual written two or three years ago probably no longer meets the organization's needs.

The following situations call for a complete review of an employee manual.[28]

- *New laws*. Federal, state, and local employment requirements change frequently. Reflect the most current laws to ensure that your organization is in compliance. Be especially vigilant in these policy areas.
  o Accommodation of disabilities. Check for changes in the definition of disability as well as changes in legal requirements.
  o Equal employment and nondiscrimination—assuming your organization is required by law to have such a policy. Check the law to determine exactly who must be included under this policy.
  o Family medical leave policies. Some organizations are required to follow only the federal Family Medical Leave Act. However, many states have additional policies for unpaid medical leave, so watch for changes in this area.
- *Company growth*. As a company grows, its employment practices change. For example, sick-leave policies and procedures for a workforce of 30 or 40 employees would differ considerably from policies and procedures for a force of three or four employees. Similarly, company growth may change manufacturing, sales, and other operations, resulting in the need for new safety procedures or travel policies.
- *Changes in benefit plans*. The changing nature of the labor force and the increasing costs of benefits prompt employers to change benefit plans, requiring revisions in the employee manual.
- *Changes in company goals and philosophy*. Acquisitions, competition, cyber security, environmental issues, employee misconduct, interest group conflicts, mergers, natural disasters, product recalls, public relations problems, and new technologies are current phenomena that usually result in a change in managerial philosophy and practice.

> • *Other changes affecting employees.* Naturally, an acquisition or being acquired, a new management team, a lawsuit brought by customers or a former employee, a physical move, a reorganization, or a workforce reduction challenges employees and may indicate changes in policy and procedures.

Note: Make minute changes as an addendum. For big changes, revise and redistribute the manual—and, again, have employees sign and return an acknowledgment of receipt, such as the one in Figure 3.10.[29]

Distribution and Design of Digital and Paper Manuals

Despite the importance of employee manuals, people generally resist reading them. Two ways to help overcome this resistance: Make the handbook both eye-catching and highly functional. In other words, apply all your report formatting and production skills to produce a manual that will be used.

Historically, employee manuals have been printed on drilled paper and the pages placed in a sturdy binder; and some organizations still distribute a printed manual. Today, though, most organizations distribute the employee manual electronically—usually on the company intranet—using a variety of software.

Employee Manual Distribution

The following list includes various methods and applications that organizations use to distribute an employee manual online.[30]

- Write and edit the policies and procedures in a word processing program, such as Microsoft Word; publish pages in PDF software, such as Adobe Acrobat Pro DC (https://acrobat.adobe.com) or PhantomPDF (https://foxitsoftware.com); and handle files with document management and storage software, such as one of these programs.
  - o OnSemble Software (https://softwareadvice.com)
  - o SharePoint (www.sharepoint.com)
  - o Simpplr (https://simpplr.com)

- Put the employee manual on a wiki, creating it in wiki software (examples follow).
    - DokuWiki (https://dokuwiki.org/dokuwiki)
    - Mediawiki (most popular) (https://mediawiki.org/wiki/MediaWiki)
    - TikiWiki (https://tiki.org/HomePage)
    Then decide whether to launch the wiki on the organization's server, which gives more control over content than launching it on a wiki farm (examples listed).
    - TiddlyWiki (https://tiddlywiki.com)
    - Wikia (www.wikia.com)
    - Wikidot (http://wikidot.com)
        Note: Chris Anderson, a policy-procedures expert and lead writer at Bizmanualz, does not recommend putting an employee manual on a wiki because "[it] can be an inefficient solution for keeping documentation up-to-date and under control." However, if you desire directions for distributing an employee manual via wiki, get them at wikiHow.[31]
- If the organization already uses a Structured Query Language (SQL) database for other purposes, investigate using it to distribute policies and procedures (examples follow).
    - AxisBase (www.axisbase.com)
    - Microsoft Office Access (https://products.office.com/en-us/access)
    - MySQL (https://mysql.com)
- Create and deliver policies and procedures to employees using a help authoring tool (HAT) program, software that develops online Help documentation from employee manual content. From a single content source, the programs listed here can generate various documentation formats (Word, PDF, HTML, and CHM [Windows Help files]).
    - HelpNDoc (https://helpndoc.com)
    - Help and Manual (https://helpandmanual.com)

o MadCap Flare (https://madcapsoftware.com/products/flare)

Programs with similar functions are available online as Software as a Service (SaaS). These applications offer the advantages of no installation or document management, accessibility anywhere on the Internet, and consulting and other services.[32] A few examples follow.

o Dynamic Policy (https://dynamicpolicy.com)

o On Policy (https://bizmanualz.com/policy-procedure-software)

o Power DMS (https://powerdms.com/)

Employee Manual Design Guides

The following design strategies will help you create a visually appealing and user-friendly employee manual.[33]

Guidelines for all manuals:

- *Keep the design simple.* Doing so enhances appearance and accessibility of the handbook and helps control production and maintenance costs.
  - o Strive for consistency throughout the manual.
  - o Omit the company logo and unusual artwork and fonts.
- *Use headings and subheadings to identify each section.* Use words in those headings that clearly describe the content, as shown in Figures 3.1 3.2, 3.3, 3.5, 3.8a to 3.8k, and 3.9.
- *Use single or multiple spacing for the paragraphs.*
  - o Place 6 to 10 points of space between paragraphs and between items or steps in a list.
  - o Put additional space (10 to 12 points) above main headings; however, keep spacing below headings the same as between paragraphs.
- *Place visuals where readers need them.* Visuals may be needed for understanding procedures. Use visuals

generously so the reader can visualize the steps and desired outcome.

- o Integrate visuals with text (at appropriate point, say "See Figure X" or "See Illustration X").
- o Make visuals easy to see and understand, separating them from the text with about 18 points (roughly 0.75 in. or 2 cm) of blank space.

- *Do not begin a policy, procedure, or paragraph of instructions at the bottom of a page* and complete it at the top of the next page. Each policy should be separate from others so that outdated policies can be removed and pages containing the new policy can be inserted easily.

- *Use a numbering system to help users find and reference specific policies.* A decimal numbering system as shown in Figures 3.1, 3.2, 3.3, and 3.9 is typical.
  - o Notice that the first-level heading carries a whole number, with the subheadings identified by decimal units.
  - o This system permits easy cross-referencing of related sections in the manual, another desirable user-friendly feature.

- *Include a preface written by the organization's president or CEO.*
  - o Summarizes the organization's objectives and philosophy.
  - o Unifies and signifies the manual's importance and theme.

- *Provide a table of contents that allows for flexibility in updating the handbook.* In a PDF file, each numbered unit in the contents list should contain a link to accelerate navigation. A sample table of contents follows.

2.0 Attendance and Time Off

2.1 Absenteeism and Lateness

2.3 Bereavement (Death in the Family)

2.5 Holiday Schedule for Employees

2.7 Hours of Work

2.9 Hazardous Weather/Emergency Conditions Plan

2.11 Leave of Absence

2.13 Family Leave

2.15 Sick Leave

2.16 Vacation

- o Some numbered units (2.2, 2.4, 2.6, and so on) are missing.
  - ▪ Thus, you can insert topics without renumbering the existing ones.
  - ▪ Example: Military leave is currently covered under Section 2.11. If that policy needs to be expanded and highlighted more prominently, the Human Resources unit could easily create a separate section: 2.12 Military Leave.
- o Page numbers are omitted from pages and table of contents for the same reason.
- o In an extremely long handbook, use primary and secondary content lists.
  - ▪ At the front, list headings of each major group, such as 2.0 Attendance and Time Off.
  - ▪ At the beginning of each section, list the individual policies in it.
- o Organize the manual by business functions or departments. Besides making a large handbook easy to use, this practice allows you to derive a separate manual for each department.
- *Put the revision date in a conspicuous place* to ensure that all employees and supervisors are using the latest version.
  - o Put the date at the bottom of the last page of each section that is changed.
  - o If the entire manual is revised, put the date on its cover.
- *Keep an authoring site and a separate publishing site.*
  - o The authoring site contains the original draft of policies and each subsequent revision, and only writers and reviewers can see it.

o The publishing site contains only the approved final version of each policy and procedure.

Guides for online manuals only:

- *Ensure an effective way to search the manual's content,* comparable to Find and Advanced Search in Adobe Acrobat Reader. The main advantage of a digital manual is its built-in search capability.
- *Provide a Help system* that allows users to type keywords or select categories of information or both.
- *Keep employees coming back to your online manual.* Consider writing a policy encouraging the staff to use the online manual rather than any potentially outdated paper copies that may be available. Consider using contests, games, puzzles, and quizzes as well as team collaboration options. Besides thinking creatively, search the web occasionally for novel ways to meet this challenge.

Guides for printed manuals:

- *Print one-sided only.*
  o This seemingly wasteful practice in fact reduces the cost of updating the handbook.
  o One-sided printing also allows the use of regular copy paper.
- *Use black ink on white paper.* Other choices may result in too little contrast between text and background. Colors may appear murky when reproduced on a copier.
- *Set standard 1-in. margins, plus a 0.5-in. gutter for drilling and binding.*
- *Begin each policy or procedure on a new page.* Thus, pages related to an outdated policy can be removed and replaced, without disturbing other sections in the manual.
- *Mark the first page of each section with a tab to help users find information quickly.*

- *Adopt a page size and binding that fits users' needs.*
  - o If it most likely will be used at a desk, the standard 8.5 by 11 size may be appropriate.
  - o If it will be used in a cramped workspace, such as an automobile or truck, a smaller size (such as 5.5 by 8 in.) may be more appropriate.
  - o Placing pages in a loose-leaf binder allows pages to lie flat and also allows for quick removal of outdated information and insertion of revised information.

Publishing and maintaining any employee manual must be an ongoing activity. A handbook is valuable only if it reflects an organization's current realities.

Summary

Everyone involved with an organization bases significant decisions on its policies procedures and instructions.

- *Policies* define an organization's perspective on specific topics and tells how related problems will be handled.
- *Procedures* tell how a series of consecutive tasks should be done. Oftentimes, procedures accompany a policy to explain how to apply it. Sometimes procedures are communicated in a flowchart, rather than text.
- *Processes* are a combination of multiple procedures involving two or more people and carried out in phases. Processes are better communicated in process maps than in text.
- *Instructions* give specific direction for doing a task and often stress correct, safe performance.

Use this checklist to ensure proper content for each kind of report.

☐ Policies contain a title, introduction, body, and conclusion.

☐ A procedure contains its purpose, scope, and definitions of unfamiliar terms; responsibilities, criteria, and quality standards; feedback required (if any) and the laws that apply; items to expedite the procedure (attachments) and helpful documents (references).

☐ Instructions contain an introduction to orient workers to the task, warnings and special notes, indication of the knowledge and skill required, the necessary equipment and supplies, and exposition of each step.

Basic guidelines apply equally to policies, procedures, and instructions.

Use this checklist to plan and then review your writing.

☐ Analyze the audience you are writing for.
☐ Identify the context (when, where, and how the policy, procedure, or instructions are to be used).
☐ Define your objective and link it to your audience and context analyses.
☐ Strive for clarity, consistency, completeness, and gender equity.
☐ For clarity, use active verbs, concrete words, and declarative sentences. Also, spell out an acronym the first time you use it.
☐ For consistency, choose one term to define an entity and use only that one.
☐ For completeness, whenever a change is made in a policy, check related policies to be sure they remain compatible.
☐ For gender equity, do not use he or him to refer to all employees or a work team.

In following best practices, take advantage of other business people's knowledge and experience. As a result, you save effort and time.

An employee manual, or handbook, is a go-to source, containing all policies and procedures of an organization.

This checklist will help you remember best practices for work instructions.

- ☐ Rely heavily on the workers who perform a task when writing, reviewing, and testing instructions.
- ☐ Consider the use of work instructions software, such as Assembly X, Ease Works, or Production Software Integrated (PSI).
- ☐ Ensure that workers have instructions always at hand.
- ☐ Make instructions clear by wasting no words and using visuals to reinforce discussion points.
- ☐ Never change written work instructions with oral directions.
- ☐ Always place each type of information—such as cautions—in the same spot.

Use this checklist to remind you of essential handbook information.

- ☐ Requirements and benefits of employment
- ☐ Attendance
- ☐ Conduct, including attire and grooming
- ☐ Confidentiality
- ☐ Definition of the terms full-time, part-time, work week, and overtime
- ☐ Earned benefits (eligibility, how to enroll, how and when to make changes)
- ☐ Grievance procedure
- ☐ Meeting legal requirements
- ☐ Nondiscrimination policy
- ☐ Performance reviews
- ☐ Personal mobile devices
- ☐ Promotion, transfer, and demotion
- ☐ Suspension and termination
- ☐ Time off (types of leave)

- ☐ Using the employer's equipment and supplies
- ☐ Additional topics
- ☐ Mission statement
- ☐ Resigning and retiring
- ☐ Travel and reimbursement procedures
- ☐ Welcome message

An employee handbook may work against an employer who ignores legal concerns in the employer–employee relationship.

Be mindful of the legal factors in this checklist.

- ☐ Before issuing an employee handbook, determine your state's requirements concerning the at-will relationship of employer and employees.
- ☐ Hire a labor attorney to review the entire employee manual.
- ☐ Include an acknowledgment of receipt in the manual and ensure every employee returns a signed, dated acknowledgement.
- ☐ Consider distributing the manual electronically for ease in referencing and updating.

This checklist may be helpful if you investigate ways to distribute your employee manual online.

- ☐ Content generated in word processing files, converted to PDF, and stored in a document management system, such as SharePoint.
- ☐ Content stored in a Structured Query Language (SQL) database, such as MS Access.
- ☐ Content generated in a Help authoring tool (HAT), such as MadCap Flare, or an SaaS version, such as On Policy.

While manual content is crucial, appearance and accessibility are important, too.

For an attractive, easy-to-use handbook, follow this checklist.

☐ Use a simple design, including headings and subheadings, single spacing, and blank space between paragraphs.
☐ Place visuals at the point of need and refer to them in your text.
☐ Do not divide policies, procedures, or paragraphs of instructions between pages.
☐ Use a numbering scheme. The decimal system illustrated in this chapter is recommended.
☐ Provide a flexible table of contents; omit page numbers and skip some numbered units in your scheme so new policies can be inserted without changing the pages that follow.
☐ Show the manual's release date on the cover for an all-new one or on selected new pages in a revised manual.

For online manuals, a search feature and Help system are critical, along with incentives to keep employees returning to the manual regularly.

The design of printed employee manuals varies only slightly from the design of other reports in manuscript format.

Use this checklist when producing a printed manual.
☐ Begin each policy-procedure on a new page.
☐ Print only one side of a sheet, using black ink on white paper.
☐ Set standard margins and add a half inch for binding— ideally a ring binder—on the left.

All stakeholders of an organization base their actions and decisions on its policies, procedures, and instructions. Therefore, whenever you contribute to these reports, you can positively affect your organization's day-to-day productivity and long-term success.

APPENDIX A

Guides for Effective, Efficient Editing

The following techniques can help you find errors in content, format, grammar, mechanics, and usage.[1]

- *Let your near-final draft rest for at least a few hours* after writing. Do tasks unrelated to your report draft. When you return to the draft, you can edit from a fresh viewpoint.
- *Check for content lapses first.* When in doubt about facts, search the Internet if doing so makes sense. Use two or three reputable websites to cross-reference information, avoiding overreliance on Wikipedia. In reports that will be posted and read online, check that all your links work and that e-mail addresses are accurate.
- *Look for the kinds of errors you are most apt to make.* If, for example, you often misuse apostrophes, proof your draft once just for apostrophes. If you tend to use the word *myself* in place of the word *me* or the phrase *for he and his family* instead of *for him and his family*, find and eliminate these problems as you begin revising. In most instances, you can use the find or search feature in your word processing software to target these lapses.
- *Read your near-final draft aloud.* Doing so accomplishes several goals. Reading audibly causes you to read more slowly and forces the brain to see mistakes and gaps that are glossed over during silent reading. And if your voice falters, you probably have found something you need to change.

- *Read your near-final draft backwards*, starting with the last paragraph and ending with the first. This disruption of the flow in your draft, forces you to pay close attention to details. Where accuracy is critical—in a new contract, for example—read each sentence backwards.
- *Check your near-final draft in a different format.* For example, make a paper copy and note edits on it; convert your text to HTML (web page); or simply change the font or font color temporarily. Increase the font size temporarily so you can see details—distinguish between commas and periods, for example.
- *Proof your text multiple times.* If you try to find all lapses in a single reading, you will likely miss some. Instead, narrow each scan to a particular kind(s) of lapse—one for content errors, one for capitalization and punctuation mistakes, one for grammar lapses, one for spelling errors and typos, and a final one for format inconsistencies.
- *Run spelling, grammar, and other checkers* at the end, because you will make changes as you proofread. This guide comes with a caveat: Proofing or checker technology is limited, with error detection rates generally in the 20% to 50% range.

Naturally, ignore absurd suggestions from your checker software. For those occasions when you are unsure about a suggested correction, keep an office reference manual handy, such as The Gregg Reference Manual, 11th edition, which is available in print and online (highered. mheducation.com).

For maximum effect, use three or more checkers on one piece of writing, starting with the tools included in your word processing software. A few other online checker options include the following:[2]

- After the Deadline (www.polishmywriting.com)
- Ginger Grammar Checker (www.gingersoftware.com)
- Grammarly (www.grammarly.com)

- Language Tool (www.languagetool.org)
- Online Correction (www.onlinecorrection.com)
- *Edit a passage again* if you changed it significantly while editing.

APPENDIX B

Manuscript Format Guides

Follow the upcoming guides to produce a report in manuscript format. A report manuscript appears in Figure B.1.

- Include at least a title page. Add other parts (table of contents, list of visuals, glossary, and so on) as needed. Observe these formatting conventions.
- Use single-spaced or multiple-spaced, blocked paragraphs unless otherwise indicated. Put a blank line above and below headings and between paragraphs.
- Use one serif font only or a serif font for paragraphs and a sans serif font for the title and Level 1 and 2 headings.
- Use a 1-in. top margin on each page after the first and a 1-in. bottom margin on all pages—usual default setting of word processing applications. On page 1, place the report title roughly 2-in. from the top and leave several blank lines below it.
- Use a left margin of 1.5 in. when binding on the left. Otherwise, make it 1-in.—same as the right margin.
- Include a title page that contains the report title, for and by whom it is written, and the report's completion date. Page borders and company logos may be added.

Producing Reports in Manuscript Format

Prepared for

Mountain View Industries
13666 E. Bates Avenue
Aurora, CO 80014

Green Mountain Ski Resort

Woodland, VT 05409 (802) 555-3265

Prepared by

KC&S Communication Consultants
Suite 116, Castle Complex
1218 Fairview Road
Denver, CO 80202

(303) 555-9154

January 2019

Figure B.1 Report in manuscript format

Source: Clippinger (2017, pp. 44–46, 73).

Producing Reports in Manuscript Format

This illustration explains one commonly used format for business reports. Notice these features of the report format: title page, margins, fonts and font styles and sizes, report headings, and spacing.

Title Page

A title page may be used to orient the reader to the report and its writer. The title page should include the report title, for whom the report is written, by whom it is written, and the transmittal date. This information, arranged in four clusters, is centered horizontally and vertically on the page.

Informative Title

To showcase the report title, type it display size (18- to 24-point font) and place it uppermost on the page. Create a concise, informative title, as follows:

- Consider the who, what, when, where, and why factors; then include the most important factors in the title.

- If the report contains recommendations that readers will easily accept, include your main recommendation in the title.

If the title you generate is too long, divide it into a main title and secondary title. On the title page, insert line breaks at logical points. An example follows.

Not this	But this
Increasing Tourism in The Hatfield-McCoy Mountains Region of West Virginia	Increasing Tourism in The Hatfield-McCoy Mountains Region of West Virginia

Optional Items

Optional items are the company logo(s), page borders, and other design elements that suggest the report content or nature of the organization. Although a title page itself may be optional in some situations, an inventive design can create a positive first impression. Therefore, use a title page to help convey your professionalism.

1

Figure B.1 (Continued)

2

Margins

Place the title 1.5 to 2 inches from the top of the first page of the report. Use a 1-inch top margin for all remaining pages. If the manuscript is unbound or stapled in the upper left corner, use a 1-inch left margin. For a left-bound manuscript, use a 1.5-inch left margin. (Staple the finished report a half inch from the left edge near the top, middle, and bottom.) Right and bottom margins should be approximately one inch on all pages.

Fonts

Use no more than two fonts in your report. This illustration, for example, uses a sans serif font (Arial) for the title and headings and a serif font (Times New Roman) for the report text. It would also be appropriate to use the same serif font for headings and report text. You may use bold and italic sparingly for emphasis. *Note:* You may need to change defaults in your word processing program to get the appearance you want.

Spacing

This single-spaced, blocked format is used extensively by contemporary business writers. All paragraphs in this example are single-spaced. To give the text a more open appearance, change the line spacing to a Multiple setting of 1.08 or 1.15 if available. Use two or three blank lines below the title, with one blank line above and below headings and between paragraphs.

Since some readers prefer a double-spaced format, always try to determine reader preference before completing the final copy of your report. If you use double spacing, tradition calls for indented paragraphs (0.5 inch) and no additional space between paragraphs.

Report Headings

Use headings in any report containing more than one major section. Headings should orient the reader to the report content.

Font style and placement must indicate the relationship of headings and subheadings. Notice that all main headings in this report have the same appearance. The subheadings are designed to distinguish them from the main headings.

Summary

Following these format guides will have two results: (1) a report that invites the receiver to read it and (2) a report that leads the reader effortlessly through its pages.

Figure B.1 (Concluded)

Notes

Chapter 1

1. The chapter focuses on internal reports—employee to manager and manager to subordinates. Therefore, the subsequent discussion of form reports purposely omits forms for collecting user information at your organization's website.
2. Smith (2015); Reyes (2017).
3. Create a fillable form (n.d.).
4. Rosenblatt (2014); Secret of Good Forms (n.d.); 3 common mistakes (2013); Input/Output & Forms Design (n.d.).
5. Clippinger (2016).
6. Clippinger (2016).
7. Clippinger (2017).
8. Shwom and Snyder (2014, p. 328).
9. Goudreau (2015).
10. Jovin (2012).
11. Galbornetti (2012).
12. Nassar (2015).
13. Earned Value Tutorial (n.d.).
14. Sharma (2017).
15. Chung (2017).
16. Chung (2017).
17. Larson and Gray (2017).
18. Scott (2016).
19. Verzuh (2015).
20. "Progress, plans, problems" (2014); "PPP: Progress, Plans, Problems . . ." (2018).
21. Gibbon (2013); "PPP: Progress, Plans, Problems . . ." (2018).
22. Gibbon (2013).
23. Gibbon (2013).
24. Lay (2015).
25. "PPP: Progress, Plans, Problems . . ." (2018).
26. Stakeholder (n.d.).
27. "Progress, Plans, and Problems" (2013).
28. Kaljundi (n.d.).
29. Fanning (2017).

30. Fanning (2017).
31. "Top 50 Prepositions" (n.d.).
32. "How to Create a Meeting Agenda" (n.d.).
33. Falconer (2015).
34. Gaur (2017).
35. Gaur (2017).
36. Formal Meeting (2013).
37. "What Type of Meeting should a Group use—Formal, Informal, or Semi-Formal" (2012).
38. "How to Create a Meeting Agenda" (n.d.); Falconer (2015); Staley (2016); Jensen (2017).
39. Bryant (n.d.).
40. McCarthy (2017).
41. McNamara (2010).
42. Harvard Business Review (2016).
43. Herold (2016).
44. Williams (2017).
45. Akalp (2014); "How to Take Productive Meeting Minutes" (2016); "How to Write Meeting Minutes" (2017).
46. "Meeting Minutes Formats" (n.d.).
47. "Art of Taking Minutes, The" (n.d.).
48. "The Insider's Guide to Effective Meetings (2013); How to Write Meeting Minutes (2017); action item (n.d.); and How to Take Productive Meeting Minutes" (2016).
49. "Supplemental Reporting and Scheduling Templates: Meeting Summary" (n.d.).
50. "How to Write Meeting Minutes (2017); Art of Taking Minutes" (n.d.); Pratt (n.d.); "Tips for Excellent Minute Taking" (n.d.); and McKay (2017).
51. "Welcome to Abbreviations.com" (n.d.).
52. "Robert's Rules of Order" (2017).
53. Robert, Honemann, and Balch with contributors Seabold and Gerber (2011).
54. "Introduction to Robert's Rules of Order" (2017).
55. Dockweiler (n.d.).
56. "You Waste a Lot of Time at Work" (2017).

Chapter 2

1. "How do you write an interview summary?" (n.d.).
2. Clippinger (2017).
3. "Focus Group" (2017); "Online Focus Group" (2016).

4. O'Brien (n.d.).
5. Shwom and Snyder (2014, pp. 159–76); Masters (n.d.); Magher (n.d.); Latham (2017); Kemp (2014); McCreery (2018); Goins (2011); Bovee (2017).
6. "About PR" (2012); "Public Relations" (n.d.); "Publicity" (n.d.); "Public Relations" (2017).
7. Duncan (2017).
8. Ferreira (2015).
9. Tapia (2017d).
10. Fleishman (2017); "Rebranding" (2017).
11. Fleishman (2017); Marx (2017); "wiki How to Write a Press Release" (2017).
12. "wiki How to Write a Press Release" (2017); Marx (2017); Fleishman (2017).
13. Definitions for the Three Terms (Buzzwords, Hype, and Jargon) adapted from Merriam-Webster Unabridged.
14. Clippinger (2017, pp. 82–86).
15. "Boilerplate text" (2017).
16. Orencia (2017).
17. Paula et al. (2018).
18. "Video News Release" (2017); Roland (2006); "Ethics in Public Relations" (n.d.).
19. Good (2008); Vincx (2014); Dickinson (n.d.); "Social Media Releases – Helpful Resources" (n.d.); Clippinger (2017, pp. 53–58).
20. "Fact Sheet" (2017); Nagy (2012); Tapia (2017c); Tapia (2017d).
21. Tapia (2017a, b, and d); B2B Tech Writer Nagy (2012); "Press Kit Elements that Work"(2006); Kennedy (2010); Nagy (2012); "Writing a Company Backgrounder" (n.d.).
22. Tapia (2017b and d); "Press Kit Elements that Work" (2006); Kennedy (2010); B2B Tech Writer (2012).
23. Paula et al. (2018).
24. Vincx (n.d.).
25. Content Marketing Institute (2016).
26. "What Is Content Marketing?" (n.d.).
27. "Visualizing Time: Beyond the Line Chart" (2015).
28. "Visualizing Time: Beyond the Line Chart" (2015).
29. "8 Tips for Building a Social Business" (2014).
30. Graham (n.d.c).
31. "White Paper" (n.d.).
32. Sailer (2017); Moore (2016); Anderson (n.d.); "What is a Landing Page?" (n.d.); Whitepaper (n.d.); Mosenson (2016); Kolowich (2017).

33. Sailer (2017); Ferrara (2013); Graham (n.d.a); Graham (n.d.b); Kantor (2015).

34. Clippinger (2016, pp. 75–83).

35. Clippinger (2018, pp. 103–05).

36. Clippinger (2018, pp. 108–10).

37. Kandler (2015); Graham (n.d.a).

38. Clippinger (2016, 101–28).

39. Null (2013).

40. McFarland (2017).

41. "Abstract and Executive Summary" (2009); "How to Write a Summary in 8 Easy Steps" (n.d.).

42. Clippinger (2018, pp. 141–58).

43. Getting an Overview (n.d.).

44. Aron (2011); Foster (2005); "Abstract and Executive Summary" (2009); Greenhall (n.d.); "Executive Summary" (2017).

45. Cox, Bobrowski, and Maher (2003); Greenhall (n.d.); Foster (2005).

Chapter 3

1. Anderson (n.d.g).

2. "Answers: Is it a Policy, Process, Procedure, or Work Instruction?" (n.d.).

3. "Answers: Is it a Policy, Process, Procedure, or Work Instruction?" (n.d.).

4. "Answers: Is it a Policy, Process, Procedure, or Work Instruction?" (n.d.).

5. "How to Do Simple Process Mapping" (n.d.); Pommer (2017).

6. "Answers: Is it a Policy, Process, Procedure, or Work Instruction?" (n.d.).

7. "What does _____ stand for?" (n.d.)

8. Kuiper (2009); Anderson (n.d.f).

9. "Answers: Is it a Policy, Process, Procedure, or Work Instruction?" (n.d.).

10. Anderson (n.d.h).

11. "ISO 9000 family—Quality management" (n.d.).

12. "About iSixSigma" (2012).

13. "Is Your Organization SOX Compliant for 2018?" (2018).

14. "Answers: Is it a Policy, Process, Procedure, or Work Instruction?" (n.d.).; Flick (n.d.a, b); Anderson (n.d.d, h); "How to Write Your First Procedure" (n.d.); Sweeny (2004); Pommer (2017); "How to Write a Standard Operating Procedure" (2018).

15. Ringel (2018).

16. "How are Employee Manuals and Operations Manuals Different?" (2017); "Give Your Employee Manual a Facelift" (n.d.).

17. Heathfield (2017a); Heathfield (2017c); "Main Components of an Employee Handbook" (2017); Murray (2018).

18. "Employee Handbook" (2018); "How to Write an Employee Handbook" (2018); Flanigan (2017).
19. Heathfield (2017b).
20. "State Requirements" (n.d.).
21. "Avoiding Booby Traps in Drafting Employee Manuals" (1996).
22. Heathfield (2018).
23. Smith (2016).
24. Grosdidier (2018).
25. "Policies and Procedures Manual Template Solutions" (n.d.).
26. "Free Policy and Procedure Template" (n.d.).
27. "12 Policy and Procedure Templates to Download" (n.d.).
28. Kuiper (2009, p. 454); Jensen (2007); Morin (n.d.).
29. Grosdidier (2018).
30. Anderson (n.d.b); "How to Start a Wiki" (2018).
31. "How to Start a Wiki" (2018)
32. "Policy and Procedures Management Software" (n.d.).
33. Kuiper (2009); Anderson (n.d.a); Anderson (n.d.c).

Appendix A

1. Clippinger (2017); Evans (n.d.); Shwom and Snyder (2014, p. 103); Vannest (n.d.); and TWL Team (2013).
2. Singla (2018).

References

"About iSixSigma." 2012. *iSixSigma.* https://isixsigma.com/about-isixsigma

"About PR." 2012. *Public Relations Society of America.* https://apps.prsa.org/ AboutPRSA/PublicRelationsDefined (accessed November 1, 2017).

"Abstract and Executive Summary." 2009. *UTS (University of Technology Sydney).* https://uts.edu.au/current-students/support/helps/self-help-resources/ academic-writing/abstract-and-executive-summary (accessed December 21, 2017).

"Action Item." n.d. *Whatis.com at TechTarget Network.* http://whatis.techtarget. com/definition/action-item (accessed August 31, 2017).

Akalp, N. 2014. "How to Properly Handle Your Company's Meeting Minutes." *Small Business Trends.* https://smallbiztrends.com/2014/09/what-are-meeting-minutes.html

Anderson, C. n.d.a. "How to Create an Effective Policy Procedures Manual." *Bizmanualz.* https://bizmanualz.com/writing-procedure-manuals/how-to-create-an-effective-policy-procedure-manual.html (accessed March 25, 2018).

Anderson, C. n.d.b. "How to Develop Intranet Policies and Procedures for Multiple Departments." *Bizmanualz.* https://bizmanualz.com/automate-policy-management/intranet-policies-and-procedures.html (accessed March 25, 2018).

Anderson, C. n.d.c. "How to Format Your Policies and Procedures." *Bizmanualz.* https://bizmanualz.com/write-better-policies/how-to-format-your-policies-and-procedures.html (accessed March 25, 2018).

Anderson, C. n.d.d. "How to Improve Your Management Procedures Usability." *Bizmanualz.* https://bizmanualz.com/write-better-procedures/how-to-improve-your-management-procedure-usability.html (accessed April 21, 2018).

Anderson, C. n.d.e. "How to Organize a Policies and Procedures Manual." *Bizmanualz.* https://bizmanualz.com/organize-your-business/how-to-organize-your-policies-procedures-manual.html (accessed March 25, 2018).

Anderson, C. n.d.f. "How to Write a Business Policy." *Bizmanualz.* https:// bizmanualz.com/write-better-policies/how-to-write-a-business-policy.html (accessed April 5, 2018).

Anderson, C. n.d.g. "What Business Policies Does Every Company Need?" *Bizmanualz.* https://bizmanualz.com/improve-company-governance/what-business-policies-does-every-company-need.html (accessed April 5, 2018).

Anderson, C. n.d.h. "What's the Difference Between Procedures and Work Instructions?" *Bizmanualz*. https://bizmanualz.com/write-better-procedures/are-procedures-the-same-as-work-instructions.html (accessed April 6, 2018).

Anderson, J. n.d. "White Papers: Pros, Cons, Examples and Best Practices." *Top Rank Marketing Blog*. www.toprankblog.com/2015/01/white-papers-pros-cons-examples-and-best-practices (accessed August 22, 2017).

Aron. 2011. "Difference Between Summary and Executive Summary." *Difference Between*. www.differencebetween.com/difference-between-summary-and-vs-executive-summary

"Art of Taking Minutes, The." n.d. *Utah Municipal Clerks Association*. www.umca.org/downloads/conferences/the_art_of_taking_minutes.pdf (accessed September 9, 2017).

"Avoiding Booby Traps in Drafting Employee Manuals." 1996. *Godfrey + Kahn, S.C.* www.gklaw.com/newsupdatespressreleases/Avoiding-Booby-Traps-in-Drafting-Employee-Manuals-1996-03-01-1.htm

B2B Tech Writer. 2012. "Five Building Blocks for the Backgrounder." http://kc-communications .com/building-blocks-backgrounder

"Boilerplate Text." 2017. *Wikipedia*. https://en.wikipedia.org/wiki/Boilerplate_text

Bovee, C. 2017. "Balancing Emotional and Logical Appeals in Persuasive Messages." *SlideShare*. https://slideshare.net/Bovee/balancing-emotional-and-logical-appeals-in-persuasive-messages

Bryant, A. March 12, 2017. "How to Run a More Effective Meeting." *The New York Times Business*. www.nytimes.com/guides/business/how-to-run-an-effective-meeting?mcubz=0

Chung, E. 2017. "PMP Earned Value Management (EVM) Calculation Explained in Simple Terms." *Edward Designer*. https://edward-designer.com/web/pmp-earned-value-questions-explained

Clippinger, D. 2016. *Planning and Organizing Business Reports: Written, Oral, and Research-Based*. New York, NY: Business Expert Press.

Clippinger, D. 2017. *Producing Written and Oral Business Reports: Formatting, Illustrating, and Presenting*. New York, NY: Business Expert Press.

Clippinger, D. 2018. *Business Research Reporting*. New York, NY: Business Expert Press.

"3 Common Mistakes When Designing Paper Forms—and What to Do About Them." 2013. *Robert Hempsall*. www.roberthempsall.co.uk/3-common-mistakes-when-designing-paper-forms-and-what-to-do-about-them

Comprose 2017. "How are Employee Manuals and Operations Manuals Different?" https://comprose.com/how-are-employee-manuals-and-operations-manuals-different.

Comprose n.d. https://comprose.com/is-it-a-policy-process-procedure-or-work-instruction (accessed April 5, 2018).

Content Marketing Institute. 2016. "B2B Content Marketing: 2015 Benchmarks, Budgets, and Trends—North America." http://contentmarketinginstitute. com/wp-content/uploads/2014/10/2015_B2B_Research.pdf

Cox, P., P.E. Bobrowski, and L. Maher. 2003. "Teaching First-Year Business Students to Summarize: Abstract Writing Assignment." *Business Communication Quarterly* 66, no. 4, pp. 36–54.

"Create a Fillable Form." n.d. *Microsoft.* https://support.office.com/en-us/article/ Create-a-fillable-form-39A58412-107E-426B-A10B-AC44937E3A 9F?ui=en-US&rs=en-US&ad=US (accessed August 3, 2017).

Dickinson, Z. n.d. "SMNR—Social Media News Release." *Realwire.* https:// realwire.com/servicesSMNR.asp (accessed November 11, 2017).

Dockweiler, S. n.d. "How Much Time Do We Spend in Meetings? (Hint: It's Scary)." *Themuse.* https://themuse.com/advice/how-much-time-do-we-spend-in-meetings-hint-its-scary (accessed September 15, 2017).

Duncan, A. 2017. "How to Create Impactful Press Kits That Work." *The Balance.* https://thebalance.com/how-to-create-impactful-press-kits-39191

"Earned Value Tutorial." n.d. *Project Engineer.* www.projectengineer.net/tutorials/ earned-value-tutorial (accessed August 18, 2017).

"Employee Handbook." 2018. *Wikipedia.* https://en.wikipedia.org/wiki/ Employee_handbook

"Ethics in Public Relations." n.d. *Wikispaces Classroom.* https://ethicsinpr. wikispaces.com/Video+news+release (accessed August 31, 2017).

Evans, D. 2016. "Proofreading Practice (or How to Avoid Those Embarrassing Writing Errors)." *GoodContentCo.* goodcontentcompany.com

"Executive Summary." 2017. *Wikipedia.* https://en.wikipedia.org/wiki/Executive _summary

"Fact Sheet." 2017. *Wikipedia.* https://en.wikipedia.org/wiki/Fact_sheet

Falconer, G. 2015. "How to Create a Professional Meeting Agenda Template." *GoToMeeting Blog.* http://blog.gotomeeting.co.uk/2015/04/22/how-to-create-a-professional-meeting-agenda.html

Fanning, P. 2017. "Abbreviated Sentences." *Guinlist.* https://guinlist.wordpress. com/2017/05/29/158-abbreviated-sentences

Ferrara, A. 2013. "3 Important Elements for Creating Effective White Papers." *Click4R.* https://click4r.com/posts/g/149036/3-important-elements-for-creating-effective-white-papers

Ferreira, C. 2015. "How to Create a Press Kit That Gets Publicity for Your Business." *Shopify.* https://shopify.com/blog/44447941-how-to-create-a-press-kit-that-gets-publicity-for-your-business

Flanigan, M. 2017. "Top 10 Reasons to Update Your Employee Handbook." *Infiniti HR Blog.* https://infinitihr.com/top-10-reasons-to-update-your-employee-handbook

Fleishman, H. 2017. "How to Write a Press Release [Free 2017 Press Release Template + Example]." *HubSpot.* https://blog.hubspot.com/marketing/press-release-template-ht

Flick, S. n.d.a. "How to Review Business Policies." *Bizmanualz.* https://bizmanualz.com/write-better-policies/how-to-review-business-policies.html (accessed April 6, 2018).

Flick, S. n.d.b. "How to Write Error-Free Procedures." *Bizmanualz.* https://bizmanualz.com/write-better-procedures/how-to-write-error-free-procedures.html (accessed April 6, 2018).

"Focus Group." 2017. *Wikipedia.* https://en.wikipedia.org/wiki/Focus_group

"Formal Meeting." 2013. *SkillMaker.* www.skillmaker.edu.au/formal-meeting

Foster, L. 2005. "Writing the Executive Summary." *York University, Toronto.* www.yorku.ca/lfoster/2005-06/soci4440b/lectures/PolicyPaperWriting_TheExecutiveSummary.html (accessed December 27, 2017).

"Free Policy and Procedure Template." n.d. *ConvergePoint.* www.convergepoint.com (accessed May 8, 2018).

Galbornetti, C. 2012. "10 Email Design Best Practices for a Mobile World." *Target Marketing.* www.targetmarketingmag.com/article/10-email-design-best-practices-mobile-email-smartphone-tablet-world/all

Gaur, T. 2017. "Run Your Staff Meeting Using these 8 Easy Steps." *Poll Everywhere.* https://polleverywhere.com/blog/run-staff-meeting

"Getting an Overview." n.d. *CRLS Research Guide.* www.crlsresearchguide.org/03_Getting_An_Overview.asp (accessed December 26, 2017).

Gibbon, C. 2013. "Planning, Productivity and Progress–The Power of P." *Cleve Gibbon.* www.clevegibbon.com/2013/01/planning-productivity-and-progress-the-power-of-p

"Give Your Employee Manual a Facelift." n.d. *Vision H.R.* www.vision-hr.com/news/3014-employee-handbook (accessed May 12, 2018).

Goins, J. 2011. "5 Persuasive Writing Tricks that Work." *Goins, Writer.* https://goinswriter.com/persuasive-writing

Good, R. 2008. "The Social Media Press Release: What Is It And Why You May Need It." *Master New Media.* http://masternewmedia.org/news/2008/05/31/the_social_media_press_release.htm

Goudreau, J. 2015. "17 Tips for Writing an Excellent Email Subject Line." *Business Insider.* www.businessinsider.com/how-to-write-an-email-subject-line-2015-1

Graham, G. n.d.a "10 Tips on Designing a White Paper." *Dummies A Wiley Brand.* www.dummies.com/store/product/White-Papers-For-Dummies.productCd-1118496922.html (accessed December 9, 2017).

Graham, G. n.d.b "For White Papers, Size Does Matter." *thatwhitepaperguy.com*. https://thatwhitepaperguy.com/white-papers-of-the-future/for-white-papers-size-does-matter (accessed November 28, 2017).

Graham, G. n.d.c "That White Paper Guy's Samples." *That White Paper Guy*. https://thatwhitepaperguy.com/white-paper-guys-samples (accessed December 8, 2017).

Greenhall, M. n.d. "Writing an Executive Summary, with Examples." *UoLearn*. www.uolearn.com/reportwriting/writingexecutivesummaries.html (accessed December 27, 2017).

Grosdidier, S. 2018. "Update Your Employee Manual." *VMC (Veterinary Medicine Consultation), Inc*. www.vmc-inc.com/post/update-your-employee-manual

"How to Do Simple Process Mapping." n.d. *gluu*. https://gluu.biz/simple-process-mapping/ (accessed April 15, 2018).

Harvard Business Review. 2016. *HBR Guide to Making Every Meeting Matter* (HBR Guide Series). Brighton, MA: HBR Press.

Heathfield, S. 2017a. "Are Employee Manuals Required by Law?" *The Balance*. https://thebalance.com/are-employee-handbooks-required-by-law-1917689

Heathfield, S. 2017b. "Need to Know What Goes into an Employee Handbook?: Here's an Employee Handbook Table of Contents for Your Use." *The Balance*. https://thebalance.com/need-to-know-what-goes-in-an-employee-handbook-1918308

Heathfield, S. 2017c. "What Does an Employee Handbook Do for You?" *The Balance*. https://thebalance.com/what-does-an-employee-handbook-do-for-you-1918123

Heathfield, S. 2018. "Sample Employee Handbook Acknowledgement of Receipt: Know the Purpose and the Reasons for Creating an Employee Handbook." *The Balance*. https://thebalancecareers.com/sample-employee-handbook-acknowledgement-of-receipt-1918900

Herold, C. 2016. *Meetings Suck: Turning One of The Most Loathed Elements of Business into One of the Most Valuable*. Austin, TX: Lioncrest Publishing.

"How Do You Write an Interview Summary?" n.d. *Reference*. https://reference.com/business-finance/write-interview-summary-3243aca53157f861 (accessed August 22, 2017).

MeetingKing. n.d. "How to Create a Meeting Agenda." http://meetingking.com/how-to-create-a-meeting-agenda (accessed August 2, 2017).

"How to Start a Wiki." 2018. *wikiHow*. https://wikihow.com/Start-a-Wiki

"How to Take Productive Meeting Minutes." 2016. *Smartsheet*. https://smartsheet.com/free-meeting-minutes-templates-microsoft-word.

"How to Write an Employee Handbook." 2018. *wikiHow*. https://wikihow.com/Write-an-Employee-Handbook

"How to Write a Standard Operating Procedure." 2018. *WikiHow.* https://wikihow.com/Write-a-Standard-Operating-Procedure

"How to Write a Summary in 8 Easy Steps." n.d. *enotes.* https://enotes.com/topics/how-write-summary

"How to Write Meeting Minutes." 2017. *MeetingKing.* http://meetingking.com/writing-meeting-minutes

"How to Write Your First Procedure." n.d. *Klariti.com Tips + Tools: Small Business Tips for Smart People.* http://klariti.com/standard-operating-procedures/14-How-to-Write-Your-First-Procedure.shtml

"Input/Output & Forms Design." n.d. *Tutorial Point.* https://tutorialspoint.com/system_analysis_and_design/system_analysis_and_design_input_output_forms.htm (accessed August 1, 2017).

"The Insider's Guide to Effective Meetings." 2013. *GoToMeeting.* http://resources.gotomeeting .co.uk/h/i/221966745-the-insiders-guide-to-effective-meetings

"Introduction to Robert's Rules of Order." 2017. *Robert's Rules of Order.* http://robertsrules .org/rulesintro.htm

"Is Your Organization SOX Compliant for 2018?" 2018. *Sarbanes Oxley 101.* http://sarbanes-oxley-101.com/

"ISO 9000 Family—Quality management." n.d. *International Organization for Standarization.* https://iso.org/iso-9001-quality-management.html (accessed April 18, 2018).

Jensen, A. 2017. "When Is the Best Time to Conduct Meetings and Important Business?" *Andrew Jensen.* www.andrewjensen.net/when-is-best-time-to-conduct-important-business

Jensen, K. 2007. "Changes That May Occur in the Workplace That May Affect Employees." *Chron.* http://smallbusiness.chron.com/changes-may-occur-workplace-may-affect-employees-18601.html

Jovin, E. 2012. "Email Salutations." *Syntaxis.* www.syntaxis.com/book/email-etiquette/anatomy-of-an-email-message/email-salutations

Kaljundi, J. n.d. "How to Write a Status Report—with a Sample Template." *Weekdone.* https://blog.weekdone.com/how-to-write-a-status-report-template-sample(accessed August 24, 2017).

Kandler, D. 2015. "Tips on How to Take Great Photos for Your Company Newsletter." *Company Newsletters.* www.companynewsletters.com/costeffect.htm

Kantor, J. 2015. "Why You Should Include Video in Your Next White Paper." *Thatwhitepaperguy.com.* https://thatwhitepaperguy.com/white-papers-of-the-future/why-not-include-video-in-your-next-white-paper

Kemp, D. 2014. "Logical Fallacy Examples." *SlideShare.* https://slideshare.net/darnellkemp71/logical-fallacies-2010

Kennedy, M. 2010. "What is a Backgrounder and Why Should PR Pros Use Them?" *e-releases.* ereleases.com/pr-fuel/what-is-a-backgrounder

Kolowich, L. 2017. "What Is a Whitepaper? [FAQs]." *HubSpot*. https://blog. hubspot.com/marketing/what-is-whitepaper-faqs

Kuiper, S. 2009. *Contemporary Business Report Writing*, 4th ed. Mason, OH: Southwestern Cengage Learning.

Kuiper, S., and D. Clippinger. 2013. *Contemporary Business Reports*, 5th ed. Mason, OH: Cengage Learning.

Larson, E.W., and C.F. Gray. 2017. *Project Management: The Managerial Process* (McGraw-Hill Series Operations and Decision Sciences), 7th ed. New York, NY: McGraw-Hill Education.

Latham, A. 2017. "How to Write a Justification Report." *eHow*. http://ehow. com/how _6375848_write-justification-report.html

Lay, J. 2015. "PPPs: A Simple System to Boost Productivity and Banish Project Chaos." *The Logbook by Hanno*. https://hanno.co/blog/ppp-plans-progress-problems

Magher, M. n.d. "How to Write a Justification Narrative." *Seattlepi*. http:// education.seattlepi.com/write-justification-narrative-6609.html (accessed October 20, 2017).

"The Main Components of an Employee Handbook." 2017. *FormSwift*. https:// formswift.com/sem/static-state/employee-handbook

Marx, W. 2017. "10 Press Release Best Practices That Will Skyrocket Your PR." *Marx Communications*. http://b2bprblog.marxcommunications.com/ b2bpr/10-press-release-best-practices

Masters, D. n.d. "Persuasive Writing Techniques: A Step-By-Step Approach." *Write to Done*. https://writetodone.com/a-step-by-step-approach-to-persuasive-writing (accessed October 19, 2017).

McCarthy, D. 2017. "10 Tips to Strengthen Your Team Meetings." *The Balance*. www .thebalance.com/how-to-lead-a-team-meeting-2275935

McCreery, L. 2018. "How to Write a Justification Report." *Chron*. https://work. chron.com/write-justification-report-6504.html

McFarland, T. 2017. "11 Electronic Signature Options and Why You Should Use Them." *Small Business Trends*. https://smallbiztrends.com/2015/06/ electronic-signature-sites-services.html

McKay, D.R. 2017. "How to Take Meeting Minutes: Keeping a Written Record of a Workplace Meeting or Conference." *The Balance*. https://thebalance. com/how-to-take-meeting-minutes-524780

McNamara, C. 2010. "Guidelines to Conducting Effective Meetings." *Free Management Library*. http://managementhelp.org/misc/meeting-management.htm

"Meeting Minutes Formats." n.d. *Meeting Minutes*. www.meetingminutes.com (accessed September 8, 2017).

Merriam-Webster Unabridged. http://unabridged.merriam-webster.com (accessed November 8, 2017).

Moore, R. 2016. "White Paper Marketing: To Go Gated or Ungated Content?" *SmartBug*. https://smartbugmedia.com/blog/gated-vs.-ungated-content-how-to-find-a-happy-balance

Morin, A. n.d. "How Often Should Your Employee Manual Be Updated?" *PEO Compare.com*. http://blog.peocompare.com/blog/bid/67119/how-often-should-your-employee-manual-be-updated (accessed May 1, 2018).

Mosenson, P. 2016. "17 Ways to Promote Your White Paper for Lead Generation." *NuSpark*. https://nusparkmarketing.com/2016/03/17-ways-promote-white-paper-lead-generation-internet-marketing

Murray, J. 2018. "Does My Company Need an Employee Handbook?: Creating a Policy and Procedures Manual." *The Balance*. https://thebalance.com/why-does-my-company-need-an-employee-handbook-398090

Nagy, J. 2012. "PR 101: Public Relations Writing." http://hotelexecutive.com/business_review/3083/pr-101-public-relations-writing

Nassar, A. 2015. "Status Report vs. Progress Report." [Blog comment.] Project Management Central. https://projectmanagement.com/discussion-topic/32405/Status-Report-vs-Progress-Report

National Oceanic and Atmospheric Administration. 2015. "Invoice Processing Procedures and Prompt Pay Guidelines." www.corporateservices.noaa.gov/finance/docs/AOD/CommercialPaymentsPresentation_7-28-15.pdf

Null, C. 2013. "E-signatures: The Complete Guide to Paperless Signing." *PC World*. www.pcworld.com

O'Brien, K. 2018. "Project Feasibility Study: Definition & Steps." *Study.com*. http://study.com/academy/lesson/project-feasibility-study-definition-steps.html

Office of Capital Projects. 2010. *Manual for Construction Project Safety Procedures*. University of Rhode Island.

Online Focus Group. 2016. *Wikipedia*. https://en.wikipedia.org/wiki/Online_focus_group

Orencia, A. 2017. "40 Press Release Examples." *FitSmallBusiness*. http://fitsmallbusiness.com/press-release-examples

"PPP: Progress, Plans, Problems—Weekly Progress and Status Reporting Methodology." n.d. *Weekdone*. https://weekdone.com/resources/plans-progress-problems (accessed August 24, 2017).

"Paper Products Manufacturing Market Global Briefing." 2018. *The Business Research Company*. https://thebusinessresearchcompany.com

Paula, F., et al., ed. 2018. *Stylebook 2018 and Briefing on Media Law*. New York, NY: The Associated Press.

"Policies and Procedures Manual Template Solutions." n.d. *Bizmanualz*. https://bizmanualz.com (accessed May 8, 2018).

"12 Policy and Procedure Templates to Download." n.d. *Sample Templates*. https://sampletemplates.com (accessed May 8, 2018).

"Policy and Procedures Management Software." n.d. *Bizmanualz*. https://bizmanualz.com/policy-management-software/policies-procedures-management-software (accessed April 25, 2018).

Pommer, S. 2017. "How to Create Visual Work Instructions." *Gluu*. https:gluu.biz/visual-work-instructions

Pratt, I. n.d. "Recording Meeting Minutes: Effective Meetings." *What Makes a Good Leader?* www.whatmakesagoodleader.com/meeting-minutes.html (accessed September 12, 2017).

"Press Kit Elements that Work." 2006. *Public Relations*. http://firoz-public-relations.blogspot.com/2006/12/press-kit-elements-that-work.html

"Progress, Plans, and Problems." 2013. *Colin Nederkoorn*. http://iamnotaprogrammer.com/Monthly-Emails-To-Advisors.html

"Progress, plans, problems." 2014. *Wikipedia*. https://en.wikipedia.org/wiki/Progress, plans, problems

"Public Relations." n.d. *BusinessDictionary*. www.businessdictionary.com/definition/public-relations.html (accessed November 1, 2017).

"Public Relations." 2017. *Wikipedia*. https://en.wikipedia.org/wiki/Public_relations

"Publicity." n.d. *Merriam-Webster*. https://merriam-webster.com/dictionary/publicity (accessed November 1, 2017).

"Rebranding." 2017. *Wikipedia*. https://en.wikipedia.org/wiki/Rebranding

Reyes, C. 2017. "Five Intranet Examples That Boost Productivity." *Liferay*. https://liferay .com/blog

Ringel, E. 2018. "Woodsmith." 40, no. 235, p. 5. *https://woodsmithlibrary.com/view/issue/235*

"Robert's Rules of Order." 2017. *Wikipedia*. https://en.wikipedia.org/wiki/Robert%27s _Rules_of_Order

Robert, III, H.M., D.H. Honemann, T.J. Balch, with contributors D.E. Seabold, and S. Gerber. 2011. *Robert's Rules of Order Newly Revised In Brief*, 2nd ed. Boston: Da Capo Press.

Roland, N. 2006. "FCC's Martin Orders Probe of TV Stations That Air Ads as News." *Bloomberg*. www.bloomberg.com/apps/news?pid=10000103&sid=aIeR2Prf88nE&refer=us

Rosenblatt, H.J. 2014. "Chapter 8 User Interface Design." *Systems Analysis and Design*, 10th ed. 320. Course Technology, Cengage Learning: Boston.

Sailer, B. 2017. "How to Write White Papers People Actually Want to Read." *CoSchedule Blog*. https://coschedule.com/blog/how-to-write-white-papers

Scott, D.J. 2016. *Project Management: A Quick Start Beginner's Guide for the Serious Project Manager to Managing any Project Easily*. North Charleston, SC: CreateSpace Independent Publishing Platform.

"Secret of Good Forms" n.d. *Select Imaging.* www.selectimaging.com/resources/the-ideas-collection/the-secret-of-good-forms (accessed August 1, 2017).

Sharma, M. 2017. "Performance Reporting." *Simplilearn.* https://simplilearn.com/performance-reporting-article

Shwom, B., and L.G. Snyder. 2014. *Business Communication: Polishing Your Professional Presence,* 2nd ed. Boston, MA: Pearson.

Singla, A. 2018. "7 Best Online Grammar and Punctuation Checker Tools for Error-Free Writing." *Blogger Tips Tricks.* www.bloggertipstricks.com

Smith, A. 2016. "Time to Update Employee Handbooks—and Sign-Off Procedures." *SHRM (Society for Human Resource Management).* https://shrm.org/hr-today/news/hr-news/Pages/CT-Updating-Your-Employee-Handbook.aspx

Smith, K. 2015. "What Can We Learn from the Millennial Mindset?" *Unity.* https://unily.com/insights/blogs/learning-from-the-millenial-mindset

"Social Media Releases—Helpful Resources." n.d. *Lint Bucket Media.* www.lintbucket.com/smr-help.html (accessed August 31, 2017).

"Stakeholder." n.d. *Business Dictionary.* www.businessdictionary.com/definition/stakeholder.html (accessed August 23, 2017).

Staley, O. 2016. "Here's the Best Day and Time to Hold a Meeting." *Quartz.* https://qz.com/653033/heres-the-best-day-and-time-to-hold-a-meeting

"In Employee Handbooks: What You Need to Know." n.d. *State Requirements. BLR®—Business & Legal Resources.* https://blr.com/HR-Employment/HR-Administration/Employee-Handbooks

"Supplemental Reporting and Scheduling Templates: Meeting Summary." n.d. *Project Management @ Loyola.* https://luc.edu/pmo/supplemental reportingandschedulingtemplates (accessed September 3, 2017).

Sweeny, P. 2004. "Four Essentials of Effective Work Instructions." *Explainers.* http://explainers.com/Articles/Four-Essentials-Effective-Work-Instructions.htm

Tapia, A. 2017a. "Backgrounder Example." *The Balance.* https://thebalance.com/backgrounder-example-1360711

Tapia, A. 2017b. "How to Write a Backgrounder." *The Balance.* https://thebalance.com/what-is-a-backgrounder-and-how-do-i-write-one-1360492

Tapia, A. 2017c. "Sample Publicity Fact Sheet for Writers." *The Balance.* https://thebalance.com/fact-sheet-sample-1360715

Tapia, A. 2017d. "What Kinds of Media Pieces Do Freelance Writers Produce?" *The Balance.* https://thebalance.com/types-of-press-materials-freelancers-must-write-1360718

"8 Tips for Building a Social Business." 2014. *Hootsuite.* https://hootsuite.com/resources/8-tips-for-social-business

"Tips for Excellent Minute Taking." 2007. *Ubiqus.* www.ubiqus.ie/writing-and-transcription/faq/tips-for-excellent-minute-taking (accessed September 8, 2017).

"Top 50 Prepositions." n.d. *TalkEnglish.com.* www.talkenglish.com/vocabulary/top-50-prepositions.aspx

Vannest, A. 2016. "5 Tips for Editing Your Own Work." *Grammarly Blog.* www.grammarly.com (accessed May 3, 2016).

Verzuh, E. 2015. *The Fast Forward MBA in Project Management (Fast Forward MBA Series)*, 5th ed. New York, NY: Wiley.

"Video News Release." 2017. *Wikipedia.* https://en.wikipedia.org/wiki/Video_news_release

Vincx, F. n.d. "5 PR Blogs You Should Be Reading." *Prezly.* https://prezly.com/academy/showcase/blogs/5-pr-blogs-reading (accessed November 20, 2017).

Vincx, F. 2014. "Visual Press Releases: A Hands-on Guide." *Prezly.* https://prezly.com/academy/content-creation/ultimate-guide-visual-press releases

"Visualizing Time: Beyond the Line Chart." 2015. *Tableau Software.* https://tableau.com/learn/whitepapers/visualizing-time-beyond-line-chart (p. 18).

"Welcome to Abbreviations.com." n.d. *Abbreviations.* www.abbreviations.com (accessed September 14, 2017).

"What Does _____ Stand For?" n.d. *Acronym Finder.* https://acronymfinder.com/ (accessed April 20, 2018).

"What is a Landing Page?" n.d. *Unbounce.* https://unbounce.com/landing-page-articles/what-is-a-landing-page (accessed December 4, 2017).

"What is Content Marketing?" n.d. *Content Marketing Institute.* http://contentmarketinginstitute.com/what-is-content-marketing (accessed December 11, 2017).

"What Type of Meeting should a Group use—Formal, Informal, or Semi-Formal." 2012. *Management Material.* http://management-me.com/2012/10/14/what-type-of-meeting-should-a-group-use-formal-informal-or-semi-formal-2

"Whitepaper." n.d. *American Marketing Association.* https://ama.org/resources/White%20Papers/Pages/default.aspx?k=contentsource:%22Main%22%20AND%20(AMAContentType:%22White%20Paper%22) (accessed December 10, 2017).

"Whitepaper." n.d. *Investopedia.* www.investopedia.com/terms/w/whitepaper.asp (accessed August 22, 2017).

"WikiHow to Write a Press Release." 2017. *WikiHow.* www.wikihow.com/Write-a-Press-Release

Williams, B. 2017. "50 Tips for Successful Meetings." *Spearmint Tips Booklets Book*, 2nd ed. 8. Kindle Edition. Vacaville, CA: Spearmint Books.

TWL Team. 2013. "25 Editing Tips for Tightening Your Copy." *Write Life Team.* https://thewritelife.com

"Writing a Company Backgrounder." n.d. *PMMI.* http://pmmi.files.cms-plus. com/uploads/Downloads/sa23E_@@_writingbackgrounder.pdf (accessed August 30, 2017).

"You Waste a Lot of Time at Work." 2017. *Atlassian.* https://atlassian.com/time-wasting-at-work-infographic (accessed September 16, 2017).

About the Author

Dr. Dorinda Clippinger earned business education degrees from Shippensburg University of Pennsylvania and Indiana University Bloomington; taught information management in Western Kentucky University's College of Business Administration; and managed titles and content development teams at South-Western Publishing Co. before founding Penworthy Learning Systems, a consultancy for publishers of instructional materials publishers. As a lecturer in management, Darla Moore School of Business, University of South Carolina, for 11 years, she taught professional communication, including report writing and presentation. For 18 years, she has been an active member of the Association for Business Communication. Dr. Clippinger coauthored with Dr. Shirley Kuiper the 5th edition of *Contemporary Business Reports*. More recently she authored *Planning and Organizing Business Reports* (2016), *Producing Written and Oral Business Reports* (2017), *Business Research Reporting* (2018), and *Business Report Guides: Research Reports and Business Plans* (2019) for Business Expert Press.

Index

OTHER TITLES IN OUR CORPORATE COMMUNICATION COLLECTION

Debbie DuFrene, Stephen F. Austin State University, Editor

- *Producing Written and Oral Business Reports: Formatting, Illustrating, and Presenting* by Dorinda Clippinger
- *Essential Communications Skills for Managers, Volume I: A Practical Guide for Communicating Effectively with All People in All Situations* by Walter St. John and Ben Haskell
- *Essential Communications Skills for Managers, Volume II: A Practical Guide for Communicating Effectively with All People in All Situations* by Walter St. John and Ben Haskell
- *How to Write Brilliant Business Blogs: The Skills and Techniques You Need, Volume I* by Suzan St Maur
- *How to Write Brilliant Business Blogs: What to Write About, Volume II* by Suzan St Maur
- *English Business Jargon and Slang: How to Use It and What It Really Means* by Suzan St Maur

Announcing the Business Expert Press Digital Library

Concise e-books business students need for classroom and research

This book can also be purchased in an e-book collection by your library as

- a one-time purchase,
- that is owned forever,
- allows for simultaneous readers,
- has no restrictions on printing, and
- can be downloaded as PDFs from within the library community.

Our digital library collections are a great solution to beat the rising cost of textbooks. E-books can be loaded into their course management systems or onto students' e-book readers.
The **Business Expert Press** digital libraries are very affordable, with no obligation to buy in future years. For more information, please visit **www.businessexpertpress.com/librarians**. To set up a trial in the United States, please email **sales@businessexpertpress.com**.

CPSIA information can be obtained
at www.ICGtesting.com
Printed in the USA
JSHW021813080320
4602JS00019B/130